How to Build a Comfortable Campsite

by

Martha Sherwood

DOMUS BOOKS

Chicago • New York

How to Build a Comfortable Campsite
Copyright © 1979 Book Developers, Inc.
Published by
Domus Books
400 Anthony Trail
Northbrook, Illinois 60062

Manufactured in the United States of America.

1 2 3 4 5 6 7 8 9 10

Library of Congress Cataloging in Publication Data

Sherwood, Martha
    How to build a comfortable campsite.

    Bibliography p. 139
    Includes index.
    1. Camping—Equipment and supplies.
I. Title.
GV191.76.S53   685'.53   78-24726
ISBN 0-089196-050-3
ISBN 0-089196-024-4 pbk.

For M.M. with affection, appreciation
and gratitude

Contents

Introduction

To those who love it wood is the first art form, a miracle in its structure, never common in its plenty. For centuries we have lived in it, walked and driven on it, slept, sat and ate from it. Cradle to coffin, wood has been our first repose and our last reward.

America's first identity was through its trees. The colonies recognized the wealth of the new land and honored various kinds of trees by emblazoning them on their individual flags. In Massachusetts Bay Colony the first coin was stamped with the form of a tree, and all early maps of America had trees drawn on them. In keeping with the religious leanings of the day, William Penn called wood "a substance with a soul."

The woods of the New World provided sustenance and cure to our ancestors. Birch bark offered oil for perfume and yellow dye. Pitch pine lampblack and butternut juice made up the first ink. The apple tree provided flavor for brandy, pie, cake, sauce, butter and candy, and its wood formed cogs, wheels, shuttles, and spoons. Holly bark cured fever and slippery elm, sore throat.

Black elder healed skin infections, and aspen bark was ground and used as a substitute for quinine.

In the 1700s traveling portrait painters reproduced the likenesses of our prairie people on wood slabs. Much of the work of our contemporary artists is done on a composition board such as Masonite which, having no pores or grain, does not shrink, expand, and crack the surface paint.

Today, trees stand representative of what the American people have become—solitary or grouped in a crowd; short, strong, and planted in poor soil; or tall and beautiful against a backdrop of grandeur. Though some are twisted and grotesque, none are ever ugly. Each, like a person, has its own way of growing and manner of being.

The age of wood was the 100-year period preceding the Civil War. It was an age of squandering. Today, the trees of this country are greedily championed by naturalist groups and protected by government regulation.

Silviculture has recently become a

national issue. An aspect of forestry, it deals with the art and science of growing trees, introducing them where they have not been and encouraging the natural forests through balancing their ecology. Silviculture makes it possible to raise wood under optimum conditions whether the purpose is commercial timber, a haven for wildlife, or to retain a beautiful landscape.

Those of us who practice our arts in the forest, whether it be survival, painting or construction, have mutual responsibilities for maintaining our national and international heritage. It will take more than a "knock on wood," that New Englander's prayer for safe keeping, to save the forests for our and our progeny's use and enjoyment. We must always be aware of our dependence on the shrubs and the giants and respect their gifts.

The following chapters take you for a ramble in the woods. There is information on fun and games and instructions in the serious business of living there. While many of the projects described in this book are ideal for weekend or overnight campers, others are meant for the person who plans to spend a great deal of time in one place—rather than for the camper or backpacker who has neither the time to spend on them nor the space to carry the tools required. In addition, some of the projects—those calling for the use of living timber, for example—are meant to be constructed on privately owned land because of their high environmental impact. What I have intended throughout is to offer a guide for those who would like to integrate with the forests, not impress their human "superiority" on them.

Before you begin looking for wood to use in the projects described in this book, you should be aware of government rules and regulations on gathering and using wood in public parks, and you should also use common sense. Always use wood from dead or fallen trees. Do not cut living branches or bark or cut down live trees or saplings.

The "Regulations Governing the Occupancy and Use of Developed Recreation Sites on National Forests" includes this rule: "It is unlawful to cut, kill, destroy, girdle, chip, chop, box, injure, or in any other way damage or remove any tree or other forest product except under permit."

Violators are subject to a $500 fine and/or six months imprisonment. It is also illegal "to construct, place, or maintain a structure, enclosure or other improvement" without a permit.

The National Forest Management Act of 1976 and subsequent regulations effective in June 1977 protect a great deal of land that is not privately owned or developed recreational property. The following rules influence the activities described in this book:

1. Individuals are allowed free use of firewood for their personal use.
2. Individuals are allowed free use of dead, insect-infested, or diseased timber, logging debris, and thinnings. Individuals may also be granted permission to use other materials when refusal of permission would cause human hardship.
3. "Free use" areas in national forests are designated by forest supervisors. In areas where dead or green timber has been marked by forest officials, it "may be cut or removed for personal use or domestic purposes." You must conduct such cuttings so as not to endanger standing timber or to threaten fire.
4. You may cut the same types of materials outside of free use areas without a permit only "in case of emergency," and you must report all such activity promptly to the district ranger. You may take "small quantities" of material needed without a

permit when you are a transient in the forest, but subject to the forest supervisor's rules.

5. You may cut green material *only* with a permit from the forest supervisor. Keep this rule in mind when contemplating a project that calls for the use of green logs or saplings.

Always check with the district ranger for additional regulations. The gathering of wood and building of fires now is prohibited in many heavily used or endangered areas of the national parks and forests.

What this all means is that, yes, the wilderness does belong to you as well as to the millions of others of us who claim citizenship in the United States. The rules are set down to protect and preserve the heritage of wood that is ours. These are our responsibilities. They are twin to our rights.

I would like to thank Ms. Diane O'Connor of the U.S. Department of Agriculture, Forest Service, for providing me with the photographs of the individual trees used in Chapter 2 and for the material outlining the Forest Service regulations of the woodlands. I would also like to thank those artists who allowed me to feature their work.

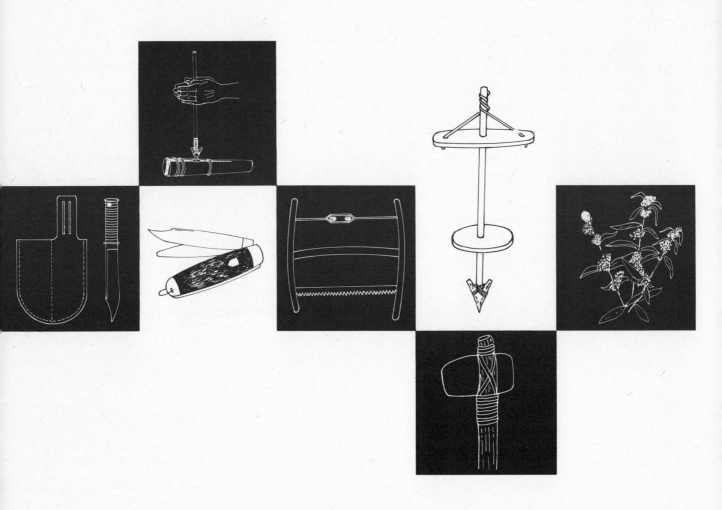

1

Gear to Get Away With

You can't get away from it all if you take it all with you. And you can't find out what you're worth if you carry the crutches of middle class comfort into the wilderness. Armed with pluck and the few essentials detailed here, you can become a deep-woods resident, making what you need out of the handy underbrush. A knife, ax (or hatchet), saw, tarpaulin and rope are the bare essentials for becoming a wilderness woodcrafter. Even some of these essentials can be replaced with what you find in the bounty underfoot and overhead.

Knives

Bigger is not better. A sharp edge and nimble fingers match and beat a machete any day. Nor does muscle and a big blade matter. A knife that is too large is not efficient in small places and is awkward and hazardous to carry. Buy the best you can afford. Avoid old army surplus and fancy imports

and look for a dependable brand and dealer who will stand behind his product. That's almost as good as having an extra hand in the woods.

The best woodcraft knives are made of high quality carbon, not stainless, steel. The 4½- to 5-inch (11–13cm) blade should be thin and tapered and the handle made of leather or wood. Because the knife is the most vital tool a New Age frontier person can have, it's a good idea to have two. One, described above, may be sheathed and worn on a belt. (A sheath may be made to your specification by a shoe repairman, or you can make your own out of cowhide or thick calfskin.) The other knife need only be a pocket variety with or without all the devices for opening cans of beer and measuring birds' nests. (Don't pay for what you won't use.) A jackknife is a good choice, with one blade for heavy work, such as cutting branches from fallen logs, and a fine, thin-honed blade—razor sharp—for special jobs. To avoid losing the pocket knife, tie a cord on the knife's ring and attach one end to your belt loop.

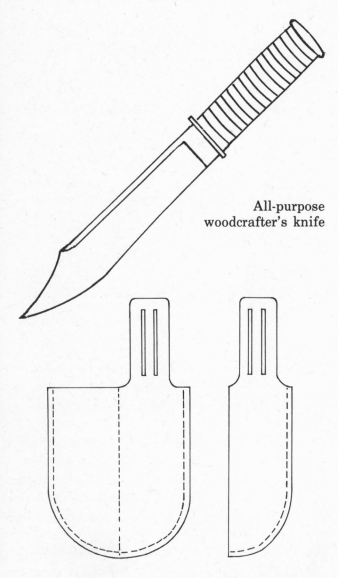

All-purpose
woodcrafter's knife

An easy-to-make knife
sheath will protect you and the tool

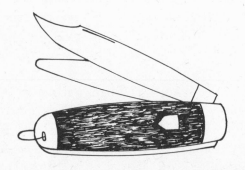

A twin blade jack-knife

Knives are tools, not playthings; so leave the target practice to circus performers who aim at brave, bikinied brunettes. If you point the thing, use it—the right way.

A sharp knife is not only more efficient, it's safer. One that is used regularly should be sharpened several times a day. Using a whetstone with a coarse and fine side, moisten the rough side and draw the knife toward you at right angles to the stone grain. Repeat three times and turn the knife over to do the other side. To fine tune it, turn the stone over, moisten and finish the sharpening on the other side. Your knife may also be sharpened with a wet handstone, rotating the blade flat in a circular motion and pressing lightly. Turn the blade over often for an even hone.

Between sharpenings keep the knife thoroughly clean by wiping it with a damp cloth. Dry thoroughly before storing. At the end of your trek into the interior or at the end of the camping season, prepare the knife for long storage by removing all rust with steel wool and coating the blade with oil or vaseline and storing it outside the sheath. (Otherwise, the coating may be absorbed by the leather, rendering it too soft to be used as protection.) The leather handle may be cleaned with shoe polish or saddle soap.

Another knife which might prove useful in pursuit of the woodcrafters' trade is the crooked knife, developed in the northern United States. One may be made at home from an 8- to 10-inch (20.0–25.0cm) long, ¾-inch (19.1mm) wide flat file, the blade of which is cut to 4–5 inches (10.16–12.7cm) and ground to a cutting edge. Using a propane or oxy-acetylene torch, the blade is then heated until red and bent down at the end in a gentle curve. The tang or handle end is fired and bent up in the same manner. To make a handle for the crooked knife, measure the tang end against a branch or root, tracing the outline. Cut a deep well in the wood and retain the shaped plug. Insert the tang, cover it with the plug, and hammer it in tight. Wrap the whole handle with wet leather thongs which, when they dry, will shrink, holding the tang in tight and giving the new knife a good grip.

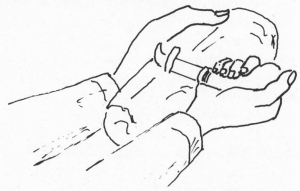

Using the crooked knife

To use, grasp the crooked knife with the palm up and the fingers closed over the top of the handle. The thumb should be along the outside curve, the butt pointing away from you. The cutting stroke is toward you. This is a right handed tool; reverse the design if you are left handed. The crooked knife may be used both as a cutting tool and as a gouge.

Axes and Hatchets

The next best thing to a trusty blade is an ax or hatchet. The first thing to determine is the size of the jobs to be done. Felling trees (which we do not advocate anywhere in this book) to build a cabin on that acre or two of land you have bought for a hideaway may call for a full ax with a 5-pound (2.25kg) head and a 3-foot (.91m) handle. But if your needs are less demanding you can get by with less than logger sized materials.

Though it is not much more efficient than a good knife and a bit more dangerous, a well-made and sharp 1 pound (.45kg) hatchet with a 1-foot (.3m) handle may be recommended for cutting small firewood or putting together some of the bigger-than-a-breadbox pieces described later.

If it is an ax you want, a 2½–3 pound (1.1–1.35kg) head with a 2-foot (.6m) handle should be the right size for splitting small logs and similarly sized jobs. The 3-pound (1.35kg) "pole ax" with a two-hand grip allows for accuracy and control. It is a bit heavy but a good trim tool.

When buying an ax, look for good quality at the best price. The ax should fit your hand comfortably and have a lively spring to it. The handle should be made of natural, unpainted, unlacquered wood with even shading. Sighting along the length, watch out for any warp which could make the ax unwieldy and dangerous. And check the grain of the wood, buying only that which has a straight vertical grain. Any other grain style has a higher chance of splitting, and an ax without a handle slows down the pleasure and progress of the outdoor experience.

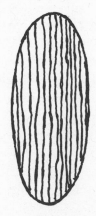

Look for a straight grain in ax and hatchet handles.

A sharp blade makes the going easier and reduces the risk of glancing blows just below the knees. To sharpen, use a constantly wet grind stone—not the power variety—and move the ax side to side against the stone. Turn the ax over often for an even hone. In camp you may use a 3-inch (7.62cm) diameter pocket stone for touch-ups or sharpen the ax using a flat file. Lean the ax against a log, sharp edge up and file down along the edge in one direction only. Fine finish with your handstone.

To use an ax, you need not be a modern day Paul Bunyon. Let gravity and the fall of the ax head do the work. Don't lean into it, and take your time. You're not going anywhere; you're already there! The best prevention of accidents is awareness of what might happen. Steadying the log to be split may result in a cleft foot. Instead, chop at an acute angle to the grain after propping the log against a larger piece of wood and approaching it from the "downwind" side. As in baseball, if you keep your eye on the spot to be struck, you're more likely to hit it directly. Practice promotes skill, so keep at it.

Axes do get broken and deserve better treatment than regarding them as dead weight in a backpack. To repair a broken ax in the backwoods, bury the ax head in the ground (to protect the edge), with the handle—or what's left of it—pointing upward. Build a fire over it and allow it to burn as long as the handle section remains. When cool, chip out the old handle. A new handle may be prepared from wood available. The best is hickory, white oak, ash, or elm. Quarter a 5-inch (12.70cm) diameter log of a length a bit longer than needed. Core one section. Shape the cored stick roughly with a knife. (Don't try to duplicate the curve; it isn't necessary.) Dry this wood piece by suspending it in the sun for 3 to 4 days. Sand it smooth and carefully split one end and wedge with a piece of shaped, dry hardwood.

To add a wedge to a wobbly handle, re-move the ax head and pry out the too-small wedge. Make a new one long, lean, and tapered. Replace the ax head and drive in the new wedge as far as possible. Put the ax to use and drive the wedge further into the space between head and handle. Saw off the protrusion.

"Care" in our careless society of easy replacement may seem an outmoded word, but in the wilderness, where the outpost is miles away, it is a vital way of life. The ax, as one of the important wilderness tools, needs to be treated well. When not in use it should not be stuck into any handy tree. To do so is to injure a living thing unnecessarily and to risk someone being struck if the ax comes loose. Also, the acids in tree bark eat away at steel if given sufficient time. Suspend an out-of-work ax in the shade (so the handle doesn't dry out) or place it flat in a dry tent. The consensus is "neither borrower nor lender be" of this important tool. It's another "natural" man-made law.

Saws

The best possible camp saw is the hard-to-come-by wood frame bucksaw which is only to be found these days in antique shops, small town hardware stores, and at country auctions. The modern version has a steel frame and collapses for easy carrying in a backpack. Joined in the middle of the arc with a steel sleeve, one end of the frame is longer than the other and serves as a handle for steadying and guiding the blade without bark-bruising the knuckles as the job gets done.

There are three blades available for this saw. The straight "V"-tooth blade is slow and a bit tough going, but as it is a wide blade it is less apt to break and is a good beginner's blade. The others are the bushman and the pulp blades.

A carpenter-like saw is another good getting-started woodcrafter's tool. It is 27 inches (69cm) long, weighs less than 2 pounds (.9kg), and comes with its own carrying case. (To improvise a saw guard when the case becomes damaged or lost, or just for extra protection, cut a piece of garden hose the length of the saw blade and split it lengthwise. Fit the guard to the blade and secure with soft wire to hold in place.)

Using either of these saws, we return to the law of logging. Let the tool do the work while you be the guide. Don't bear down, but with easy, smooth strokes, let the saw's own weight cut its way home.

Modern camp craft manufacturers have come up with a backpack saw that is easily packed and can be used for cutting small pieces of firewood. It is the ½-ounce (14g) wire saw which can be used as is or in conjunction with a curved, forked branch. Be sure to make a thick case to carry this tool as its twisted teeth can shred a nylon pack pronto.

If you're going to be in a set camp for several days it might be worthwhile to build a simple sawhorse to make your work even easier. Prepare four stakes, 3 feet (.9m) long and about 4 inches (10cm) in diameter. Sharpen one end of each with an ax or your knife. Setting a 10- to 12-inch (25–30cm) diameter log on the ground, straddle it with the two crossed sticks at either end, like an "x" over "o's," driving the stakes firmly into the ground. The two stake sets should be no more than 2 feet (.6m) apart. You may or may not want to secure the middle of the crossed spikes with a cord. It's optional. Rest the log to be cut between the uprights. This sawhorse is capable of supporting almost any log weight.

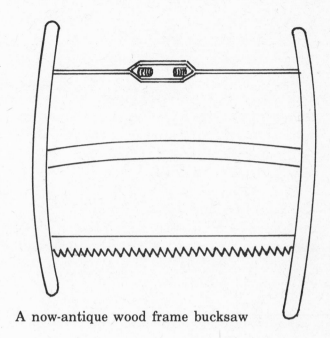

A now-antique wood frame bucksaw

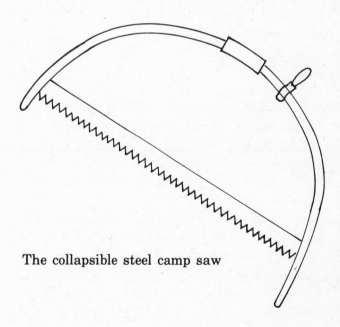

The collapsible steel camp saw

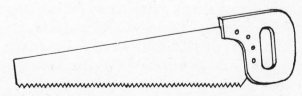

The carpenter's saw: a basic woodcraft tool

Camp sawhorse

Tarpaulin

The versatile tarp doubles as a shelter for rainy day picnics, a ground cloth for sleeping outdoors, and an architecturally diverse shelter. Several tarps lashed together can raft a small party and gear across or down a stream.

Tarps come in assorted sizes and colors. In polyethylene you may get an 8 × 9 foot (2.4 × 2.7m) tarp which weighs 1 pound, 8 ounces (.674kg); a 9 × 12-foot (2.7 × 3.6m) one at 2 pounds (.90kg); and a 12 × 12-foot (3.6 × 3.6m) model weighing 3 pounds (1.35kg). Some cloths may have triangular-shaped ends which can be used as tent door flaps. Grommets (eyelets) along the sides can be used for staking the tarp to the ground. If you find a tarp that doesn't have grommets, you can purchase vinyl tape with grommets at one end which are adhesive and stick to plastic tarps. Some plastic tarps also come with ties to which you can attach nylon cord at any of many points, providing great versatility.

To make your own tarpaulin, you may choose from a number of fabrics. Muslin, which is lighter than canvas, can be bought from a local yardgoods store for a nominal cost. You may have it waterproofed and ask a local canvas store to put grommets 18 inches (.3m) apart along all of the sides.

Other materials which can be used are:

Duck—which weighs 10.1 ounces (303g, approximately) per square yard and is very durable. All cotton duck is good, but you may find it reinforced with nylon or Dacron. It needs periodic waterproofing.

Drill—which is a common, diagonally woven tent material. If there is evidence of a high starch or sizing content, be aware that this might be replacing real weather-proofing.

Poplin—a light and durable, wind and waterproof material which weighs 6 ounces (168g) per square yard.

Nylon—the lightest of all at 1½ ounces (42g) per square yard. You can get nylon coated on two sides with vinyl, providing a tough waterproof cover. Nylon's negatives are that it is slippery and frays badly. Check the edges of a nylon tarp to see that they have been melted to fuse the yarn. You may remedy any oversight at home with a very hot iron.

A homemade tarp may be constructed easily using three 12-foot (3.6m) long, 32-inch (80.0cm) wide strips of waterproofed fabric. Remember, the heavier the fabric the greater the abrasion and tear resistance and the longer it will last. But, it also will be heavier to carry. Sew the strips together lengthwise and hem. The corners should be reinforced with 4-inch (10cm) square pieces of material, and the edges where grommets or tapes are to be set should be reinforced using a 2 × 4-inch (5 × 10cm) piece of material. (Tapes are easily made using 2-foot (50cm) long pieces of twill folded in the middle where they attach to the tarp. Half-inch (12.7mm) grommets should be added to each corner and midway along the sides. In addition, inset grommets again half way between the holes on the long side.

The cheapest tarp tent to make or buy is called the "forester." It is easy and quick to pitch using three poles and eight pegs and warms rapidly with a fire in front. Triangular in shape, the forester can sleep one person or a cozy couple. For the best space accommodations, set it up with a peak of 6

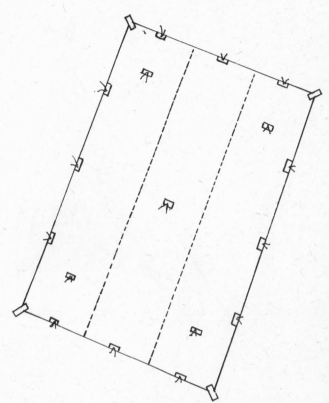

A homemade tarp with tapes

feet (1.8m) off the ground in the front and 3 feet (.914m) at the rear.

Do-it-yourselfers can make their own waterproofing mixtures or purchase a commercial variety through a camping equipment company. To make your own, grate laundry soap into hot water, allowing one large bar to a gallon. Stir the mix to dissolve the soap. Make up a mixture of ¼ pound (.1kg) alum (available at the pharmacy) to a gallon of hot water (or enough to cover material).

First soak the canvas or other material in the soap solution and hang it up to drip dry. Then soak it in the alum mix overnight and wring out and dry.

A wax waterproofing solution can be made of one pound (.45kg) of paraffin shavings added to a gallon (3.8l) of turpentine. To speed the melting of the wax, set the con-

A variation of a tent for one or two persons

tainer in hot water. *Do not heat.* The mixture is highly flammable. Stake the tarp out in the sun and while both the tent material and the waterproofing solution are warm, paint the fabric. Allow the tarp to remain there until it is dry.

Another outdoor, on-site solution to waterproofing is to brew up oak or birch bark in water and allow the tarp to soak in it for two days. Allow it to dry fully before using.

The quickest way to waterproof fabric is to rub an ironed canvas with a block of paraffin until the cloth shows white; then iron with a warm iron to set.

Rope and Cord

So you've got all of this loose wood around, propped up against trees, stacked for fire. Without cord of some kind to give these big sticks form, wood's use just about ends at the fireplace.

The final woodcraft tool to be brought from home is rope, left long and kept dry. The best selection is manila hemp, which is strong but hard on the hands. The next is sisal, which is less expensive but weaker and less durable. Cotton, as in clothesline, comes next. Smooth, but hard to handle when wet, it takes on a freeform all its own when frozen. Nylon is the last choice. Although it's hard and strong, it's also expensive, slippery, and stretches with use.

To transport rope into the bush, form it into a coil, using thumb and elbow as guides, and carry the coil over the shoulder. When there, you will be able to determine the lengths needed and cut with your knife accordingly. Be sure not to cut your pieces too short unless the lengths will be used permanently, as in pegging a tarp, for example. To keep cut ends from unraveling you may wrap them with electrical tape or dip in glue and allow to dry.

Like all woodcraft tools, rope needs maintenance and care. If it gets wet, it should be allowed to dry thoroughly before it is coiled loosely and stored. The best storage method is to hang it in a well ventilated spot. Rope is a prime target for the gnawing of rodents, porcupines, and squirrels, so watch where you put it.

Making Tools

Now you've gotten there, beyond the highways and away from it all . . . including away from some of the handy tools you didn't have room for, didn't think you would need, or inevitably forgot when you packed your rucksack. Now what? You can make do or make your own. The following items are handy to have in the outward bound tool kit and fun to make, to save, or to use and leave behind.

Pump Drill: A variation of the Indian fire stick provides a tool for boring holes in wood, leather, or bark. This tool is still being used by the Indians of the Southwest to bore holes in turquoise. The shaft of the drill is made of a peeled sapling or a whittled down stick of well-seasoned hardwood 18–24 inches (45.0–60.0cm) long. The stick should be tapered from ⅜ inch (9.37mm) diameter at the top to ½–¾ inch (12.5–18.75mm) at the bottom. The upper end should be horizontally notched narrow enough to pinch the string. The shaft should be sanded smooth. If it is warped, warm the stick over a fire and hold it bent against the warp to straighten it. Attach a two-direction ¼ inch (6mm) diameter drill bit from the hardware store, an arrow head if you are lucky enough to have one or skilled enough to make one, or a headless nail to the end of the shaft.

A slab of wood or a flat stone may be coaxed into service as a flywheel. Saw a small log or tree branch crosswise to form a flat ¾ inch (18mm) thick disc, 4–6 inches (10–15cm) in diameter. A perfect circular shape will allow the drill to run smoothly. Drill a hole in the flywheel's center large enough to receive the narrow end of the shaft and large enough for the flywheel to move down the shaft to within 3–4 inches (7.5–10cm) of the tip. (You may want to notch the shaft to stop the flywheel where you want it.) The perfectly horizontal positioning of the flywheel to shaft will also allow the drill to run properly.

The third vital part of the pump drill is a flat, oval wood bar or "bow board" positioned 4–5 inches (10–12.5cm) above the flywheel. It may be made of any wood 8 inches to 3 feet (20–90cm) long (about one-half the length of the drill shaft). The best bar is made of a flat stick ½–1 inch (1.25–2.5cm) thick. A hole is bored in its center only a little larger than the shaft above the flywheel.

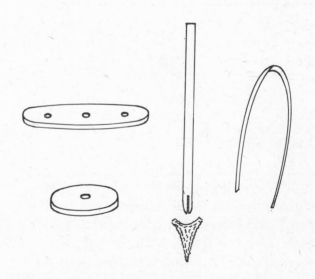

Pump Drill parts: bow board, flywheel, drill stick and bit and the leather thong to turn it

To assemble the pump drill, tie one end of a strong, thin, limp cord (leather thong) to one end of the bow board. Insert the shaft, thread the cord over the notch at the top of the shaft and secure it at the other end of the bow board. Strung in this way the bow board should rest 2–3 inches (5–7.5cm) above the flywheel.

tom; let up the pressure and the string will rewind itself around the shaft in the opposite direction. Continue to press down and release the drill until the hole is drilled allowing the speed of the drill to do the cutting, not pressure from your hand.

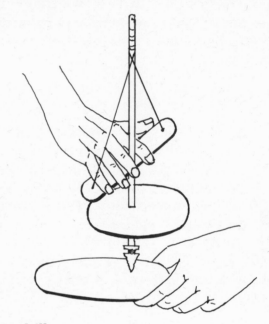

Pump drill

Assembled pump drill

The drill is operated by holding the right hand flat to the bow board with the shaft set between the index and middle fingers. Twist the shaft with the left hand to wind the string around the shaft several times. Holding the shaft absolutely vertical, but at the point to be drilled, push the bow board down evenly until you reach the bot-

For a more simple hand drill, use only the drill rod with the attached point. Rotate between the palms of the hands to drill the holes you need.

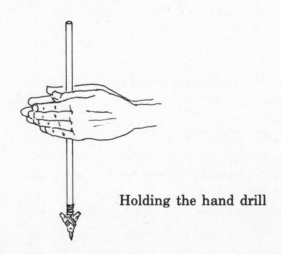

Holding the hand drill

Vise: To hold an object steady while drilling, you will need a third hand—in this case a made-on-the-spot vise. Split a thick stick at one end using a sharp knife. Bind the end just at and below the split with wet leather thongs to prevent its splitting further. Insert the object to be drilled between the splits and bind the open ends together with more thong.

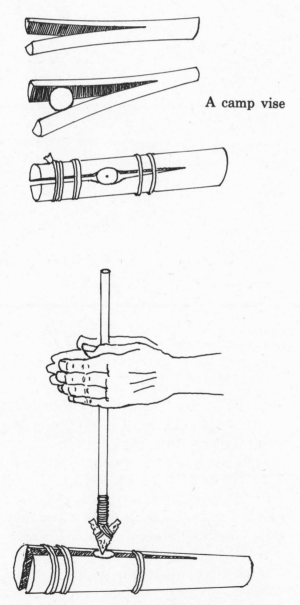

A camp vise

Boring a hole in a securely held piece of wood.

Lashing Materials

Cording is last on the list of necessities, not because you won't need it but because it's the most easily improvised woodcraft tool. The inner bark of basswood, American elm, hickory, white oak, osage orange, buckeye, and red cedar provide the cordage for making rope and twine. (See Chapter 2 for tree identification specifics.) Basswood, the favored tree bark cording, makes a lighter, smoother, and easier to handle rope than that commercially available. It is also the best source for string and vegetable thongs. Actually, any fibrous material may be used that is long (12 to 24 inches; 30 to 60cm), strong, and flexible. Other natural cording materials are surface roots, ground vines, long grasses, reeds, and rushes. Even seaweed can be coaxed into cording for palm frond huts.

While there are lots of ready-made lashings available in the woods for that project needed immediately at the campsite—vines and surface roots that can be improvised into effective lashings—it is also fun to try your hand at rope-making. It does, however, take a number of days (sometimes weeks) to complete some of these projects, so this is not for the fast-traveling backpacker.

Preparation: Look for a fallen tree of one of the above varieties. Making long, narrow horizontal cuts (in the direction of the tree's growth) pull off sections of bark. Soak these sections in water for 7 to 10 days, then separate the inner from the outer bark. Thin strands may be made by bending the bark and separating at the edges with a knife or fingernail.

Make a lye water solution by boiling wood ashes in water for 10 minutes and pouring the water into another pot. Immerse the bark strands in the wood ash water and boil occasionally over a 24-hour period. To separate further, hang the bark over a pole and pull on either end.

A cord is only as good as its strength. There are ways to determine whether what you make with the above materials will hold up under the weight of wind, weather, or the human body. The first test is to simply give your cord a straight yank. If it breaks it will not stand up to 60 to 80 pounds (27–36kg) of pressure, much less more. Twist the cord to test it a second time for strength. Pliability may be determined by tying the cord in a knot and pulling it tight. Again, if it breaks, the cord will be worthless for your woodcraft purposes.

To give you an idea of the relative strengths of some natural fibers, bark fiber rope of 1-inch (2.5cm) diameter can withstand 500–1,500 pounds (225–675kg) of weight. A green grass rope of the same diameter will hold 100–250 pounds (45–112kg) of weight. And coarse grasses (sedges) are rope giants able to hold 2,000–2,500 pounds (900–1,125kg) of weight.

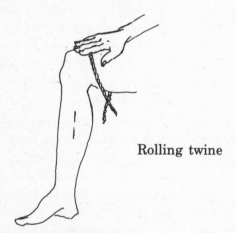

Rolling twine

Twine: To make twine ⅛–¼ of an inch (about 3–5mm) wide, roll two strands in one direction along the thigh. Cut ends unevenly and splice another strand end-to-end with the short cut as needed. Continue rolling and splicing until you have the desired length needed.

Rope: To make rope for heavy duty woods jobs, take the strands of the inner bark after soaking. Use a group of strands that is one-half the thickness you want for the finished product, and hang over a short, low tree limb or nail. One end should be a foot (.3m) shorter than the other. Taking one strand in each hand just below the nail,

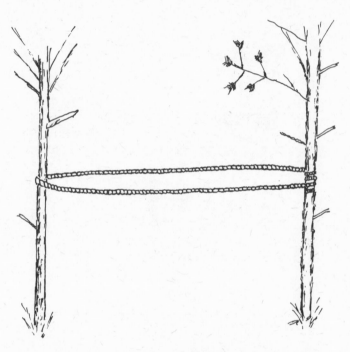

Stretching rope to dry

twist left to right, changing hands and repeating, splicing new strands to the short ends of the forming rope until the necessary length is reached. To finish, stretch the new rope between two sturdy saplings situated half as far apart as the rope is long. Tie one end to the first sapling, walk it around the other, and tie the second end to the original tree. Untie the rope from the trees and re-stretch three to four times a day. In two days the rope will be dry. Remove it from its rack and trim the tufts.

Other plants which lend themselves to cord making are:

- Indian hemp (Apocynum cannabinum). The inner bark is collected in the fall. Soak full bark in water until the inner bark separates into fibers resembling brown silk. Roll into twine.

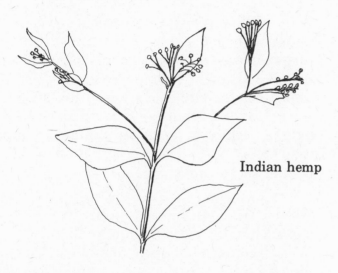

Indian hemp

- Common and Swamp Milkweed (Asclepias incarnata L.)

Milkweed plant

- Nettle (Urticastrum divaricatum). Gather the dried stalks of this prickly plant in the fall and soak as previously described. Nettle may also be used green to make fish nets. In this form it is 50 times stronger than cotton twine.

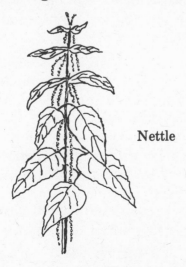

Nettle

Milkweed pods

- Yucca (Yucca baccata). Found in the desert of the Southwest, the leaves of the Yucca are soaked, then pounded with a rock while being rinsed frequently. The remaining fibers are combed and rolled into cord.

- Reed grass (Phragmites communis Trin.) A Pacific Coast plant, the psoralea reaches 12 feet (3.65m) and sports purple spiked flowers. The inner bark and the plant's roots are used to make a scented "string."

- Bulrushes (Scirpus vilidus).

Root Rope: Cording can also be made of the rootlets of the white spruce, hemlock, tamarack, balsam fir, cedar, cottonwood, and long-leaf, digger and yellow pine trees. Gather and soak the trailing roots of these trees in hot water. Scrape off the outer bark and halve or quarter the larger-than-pencil size roots. (Instead of water soaking, roots may be buried in hot ashes for an hour.) Roots may be used as is or saved for future use, soaking in water to regain pliability.

Withes, for cording made of green shoot fiber, are easy to obtain and strong enough to "wire" together a log raft. Select the tall shoots of the hickory, white oak, black ash, birch, wild raisin, willow, sweet gum, witch hazel, or chestnut tree. But *do not cut.* Instead, grasp the end of the shoot twisting and pulling to loosen it into strands. Bend and tie at one end with a binder knot achieved by twisting the ends around one another. If the fibers don't loosen easily you may cut the shoot and, laying it across a log, pound on all sides with a rock, one end to the other. Then using a foot to anchor the shoot at one end, twist as before.

Other Hand Tools

As usually happens when a person gets involved in any activity, the tools used at first are soon inadequate. The following are several items which can be made on-site as the needs arise.

Glue: When a lash will not hold and a wedge will not do, glue. Boil together a mixture composed of 85 per cent resin from a spruce, balsam fir or pine tree and 15 percent bacon fat. Or boil the heads, fins and tails of several fish in water until all that is left is a sticky substance. These glues can be used to secure stool pegs or any other job calling for an adhesive.

Hoe: Although you are not likely to plant a garden in the woods during your stay, a hoe can come in handy for digging drainage ditches, latrines and any other sort of large hole. Locate a dead hardwood branch 4–6 inches (10–15cm) thick. Cut it at the point where a 5–6 foot (1.5–1.8m) long 1½ inch (3.75cm) thick branch comes away at a wide angle. Cut the hoe head out of the main branch and trim the side branch smooth to form the handle. Sharpen the edge of the new hoe with a knife and fire-cure it to harden.

Mallet: Contrary to common practice, it is not wise, either from the standpoint of safety or care of the tool, to use an ax head for a hammer. Instead, cut a 2-foot (.6m) section of limb from a green hardwood tree (oak or hickory). Whittle two-thirds of the length into a handle with your ax and smooth it with your knife. Allow it to cure before using to split logs or any other major camp job requiring a bludgeon.

Tomahawk: The Algonquin Indians named this handy woodland tool and used it in conjunction with fire to cut down trees. In contemporary camps the tomahawk may be used anywhere a hatchet is handy. Chip both ends of an oval piece of flint, quartzite, obsidion, jasper, or volcanic glass into sharp edges with a flat piece of stone. Notch the stone in the center at the top and bottom. Cut a hickory sapling 18–24 inches (45–65cm) long and whittle one end of it to form a long bark "tongue." Soak the tongue in boiling water to make it flexible and fold it around the notches in the stone. Lash the tongue to the stone with a crisscross of leather thongs.

Wedges: These are the log splitting tools. Hewn out of 18-inch (45cm) long and 4–6 inch (10–15cm) thick sections of hardwood limbs into wide pie shapes, wedges are cured and are mates to axes in dividing timber in half.

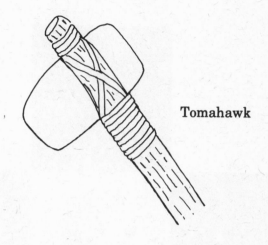

Tomahawk

Now, off you go, to see the forest *and* the trees; to make way in the real world, son or sister of the Indian. The first natural law is take nothing you don't need. Make do with fallen trees and wood scraps so there'll be some for the nature hunters who follow and for when you return again to the great, green outdoors.

2

Tree Identification

It all begins with trees. Until you begin to discern the subtle and not-so-subtle differences between the barked columns around you, all trees look much alike: large or small, with needles or leaves, dead or alive. But you must become a bit choosier if you are going to call them neighbors for any length of time.

Basically, there are two types of trees—the broad-leafed variety, which are hardwoods with large leaves such as oaks, maples and basswood, and the conifers, those with needles rather than leaves and which bear cones. (In fact, the conifer trees themselves often are conical in shape.) These conifers—pines, firs, spruces—dominate the cold climates of the hemisphere and also are known as evergreens.

The North American continent may be divided into six timber belts based on varied latitudes and climatic differences. There is some blending at the edges as some trees thin out and others begin to appear. But the best way to know the territory in which a

tree will appear is to know its soil and climate preferences.

The northern forest belt, which incorporates New England, the upper Great Lakes (to Minnesota), Canada, and Alaska, is dominated by such conifers as the white and black spruces, balsam fir, eastern hemlock, the eastern white, red and jack pines and the tamarack, to name a few. The broadleaf trees appearing there are the birches, sugar maple, oaks, the quaking and bigfoot aspens and the American beech and elm.

East of the Great Plains and southwest from New England through Georgia to Texas and the Lower Mississippi Basin is central hardwood country. Due to even rainfall, variable weather and rich soil, the black walnut, American sycamore, yellow poplar, yellow buckeye, oaks, maples, ashes, hickories, and basswoods flourish.

The southern forest and the southeastern woods, which are sandy and dry, boast the shortleaf, longleaf, loblolly, and slack pines and the bald cypress. To soften the contrast are the magnolias, tupelos, hickories, oaks, and hollies. This rich mix is found from Virginia to Florida and west to Texas including Mississippi, Louisiana, Georgia, and Alabama. The subtropical lands at the tip of Florida and the mouth of the Rio Grande River in Texas host trees which are foreign further north—West Indian mahogany, mangroves, and various species of palms. Cedar, citrus, rosewood, and even pines are also found in this Caribbean suburb.

High in the slopes of the Rocky Mountains where winds blow cold and long and the growing season is short and sweet, the conifers dominate. In a belt from Canada to Mexico grow Douglas, Colorado and white firs, white, yellow and ponderosa pines, spruces and larch.

At land's end, along the Pacific from Alaska to Northern California, is the last timber belt. Here in the mild climate and under ample rain, the broadleaf trees grow at low elevations, and the conifers hold forth. Western and mountain hemlock, cedars, pines, juniper, cypresses, and the redwoods and giant sequoias stand patiently to pose for a picture postcard.

The following trees are those which figure most prominently in the art of woodcrafting. They are referred to in following chapters with regard to fire building, shelter, and craft projects. Also included in the identification data are those animals attracted to specific trees. This is offered for the purpose of observation, photography or survival hunting, as you choose. As hunters are said to first respect the lives of the wilderness creatures because of their intimate knowledge of their game, so a deep knowledge of trees will no doubt seal your respect for these stationary beings.

Autumn leaves and catkins of the red alder

Alder (Alnus)
  Leaves: Irregular teeth; shallow lobes; oval to oblong; prominent veins; cone-like strobiles (multiple fruit) ½–1³/₁₀ inches (1.24–3.25cm) long.
  Buds: Red-brown and scaley.
  Location: Moist soil; northwest part of U.S.; also extends south from Arizona and Texas into Mexico; seaside alder (Alnus Maritima) sporadically seen in above locale. Eight species in U.S. and Canada.
  Wood: Good for quick, hot cooking; best used dry. Gives forth with a noisy, sparky fire.

Alder, European (Alnus glutinosa)
  Leaves: Broad; wide in middle; coarse teeth. Young leaves are gummy.
  Bark: Dark, warty stripes.
  Location: Wet soil; Newfoundland,

Illinois to Delaware and Pennsylvania.

Size: 50–70 feet (15–21m) tall; 1–2 feet (.3–.6m) in diameter.

Apple (Malus)

Leaves: Alternate; toothed.

Flowers: Blossoms with fragrant white or pink clusters, 1–1½ inches (2.50–3.75cm) in diameter.

Fruit: Varies from tiny and tart to large, round, sweet, and juicy; greenish yellow to red.

Location: Spread through U.S. and southern Canada.

Note: That which we know as "apple" was naturalized by the settlers and is a common southwest European and Central Asian variety. It originated, it is speculated, in the western Himalayas.

Animals attracted: Deer, pheasant, mourning dove, and gray fox, to name a few.

Ash, White (Fraxinus americana)

Leaves: 8–12 inches (20.25–30.0cm) long; oval to oblong leaflets; may be smooth or have a fine serration.

Bark: Gray with diamond shaped ridges; dark, tight on older trees.

Flowers: April to June.

Location: Inhabits the upland woods of Nova Scotia, southern Quebec, southern Ontario, northern Michigan, southeastern Minnesota to Florida and eastern Texas.

Size: 80 feet (24m) tall; 3 feet (.914m) in diameter.

Wood: Considered the most valuable and largest native ash, this tree provides hard, strong, and durable wood for furniture, oars, tool handles, and snowshoes. As campfire material it equals oak and hickory. Offering little smoke,

it burns green or seasoned. Wood is straight grained; has no flexibility; splits easily.

Pistillate flowers of the white ash

Fruit of the white ash

Bark of the white ash

Twig of the bigtooth aspen

Fruit of the bigtooth aspen

Leaves of the bigtooth aspen

Fruit of the quaking aspen

Aspen, Bigtooth (Populus grandidentata)
  Leaves: White; woolly on underside when young; large leaf teeth; grown in 5–15 pairs.
  Bark: Dark green on young trees, brown and furrowed on older trees; smooth, yellow-green also common.
  Location: Prefers dry soil; Novia Scotia, eastern Quebec, Ontario, southeastern Manitoba to Maryland in the U.S., western Virginia, western North Carolina, Kentucky, western Tennessee, northeastern Iowa.
  Size: 30–40 feet (9–12m) tall; 1–2 feet (.3–.6m) in diameter.
  Wood: Green or dry, it is easy to chop; light, it splits with ax stroke. Burns well seasoned, nearly smokeless. Beavers prefer the poplar family, so finding a tree with teeth marks may be as good as identification of the leaves.

Aspen, Quaking (Populus tremuloides)
  Leaves: Almost circular, 1–3 inches (2.50–7.75cm) long. Shows 20–40 pairs of rounded teeth; green on top, pale silver beneath. (This gives the tree a shimmering effect as it moves in even the slightest breeze.) Brilliant gold in fall.
  Bark: Green-white or cream; black warty spots; thin and scaly.
  Location: Found in the dry woods of Newfoundland, Labrador, Alaska to New Jersey, northern Virginia, and West Virginia, Ohio, northeastern Missouri, eastern South Dakota, southwestern Nebraska, Colorado, western Texas and southern California.

Basswoods (Linden tanulia)

Leaves: Simple; alternate; broad and oval with coarse-toothed margins.

Flowers: Creamy white; develop into a nutlike fruit.

Location: Northern Hemisphere; four species in eastern U.S.

Wood: A good cordage tree; Asian cousin is the source for jute.

Basswood, American (Tilia americana)

Leaves: Largest of variety; 5–6 inches (12.75–15.25cm) long; 3–4 inches (7.75–10.25cm) wide.

Bark: Dark gray on older trees; ridged and furrowed.

Flowers: Have honey flavor.

Location: Moist woods; New Brunswick, southern Quebec, Manitoba to Florida, Texas.

Size: 60–80 feet (18–24m) tall; 2–3 feet (.6–.9m) in diameter.

Wood: Easy to split; best used dry for kindling; makes slow fire with coals. Soft wood, it decays very quickly.

American basswood tree in winter

American beech

European beech

Beech, American (Fagus grandifolia)
 Leaves: 2–6 inches (5.0–15.25cm) long;
   1–2½ inches (2.50–6.25cm) wide.
   Smooth surface; slightly hairy under-
   neath; small teeth.
 Bark: Blue-gray; blotching is common.
 Fruit: Small, edible nuts in triangular
   shape appear September and October.
 Location: Rich, mature soil with ample
   surface moisture; Nova Scotia, Prince
   Edward Island, and southern Ontario.
   In the U.S., eastern Wisconsin to
   northern Florida and Texas.
 Size: 60–100 feet (18–30m) tall; 2–3 feet
   (.3–.9m) in diameter.

 Wood: Easy to split when green; difficult
   when seasoned. Burns well dry or
   seasoned, making good coals. Good for
   forest furniture, tools, and fuel.
 Animals attracted: Pheasant, bobwhite,
   wild turkey, ruffed grouse, black bear,
   red and gray fox, raccoon, whitetail
   deer, cottontail rabbit, squirrel, opossum, and porcupine.

Beech, European (Fagus sylvatica)
 Leaves: 2–4 inches (5.0–10.25cm) long;
   rounded teeth; hairy veins and margin.
 Bark: Darker than American.
 Note: This is a European timber tree
   which is mainly ornamental in the U.S.

Birch (Betula)
   Leaves: Double toothed; egg-shaped or triangular.
   Bark: Crossed with streaks; papery.
   Flowers: Catkins (fuzzy, caterpillar-like cluster of drooping flowers).
   Wood: Highly inflammable bark even when damp; used to make clothespins, spools, woodenware, cabinets, novelties; decays quickly, splits easily and easy to chop; smokes cooking pots.
   Note: There are 40 species, small to medium in size.

Yellow birch (Betula alleghaniensis)

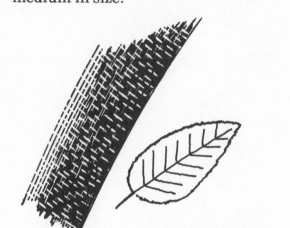

Black birch and leaf

Birch, Black (Betula lenta)
   Leaves: 1–6 inches (2.5–15.25cm) long.
   Bark: Brown or black; thin horizontal striping.
   Flowers: April through May.
   Location: Mature forests; Great Lakes and Appalachian areas, southwestern Maine, southern Quebec, eastern Ontario to Delaware, Maryland.
   Size: 50–70 feet (15–21m) tall; 2–3 feet (.6–.9m) in diameter.
   Wood: Hard; heavy but easy to split when green. Good for furniture making.
   Animals attracted: Grouse, deer, moose, rabbit.

Birch, Yellow (Betula lutea)
   Leaves: 1–5 inches (2.5–12.75cm) long.
   Bark: Shiny; yellow to silver gray; narrow, horizontal lines peel in thin curls.
   Flowers: Spring.
   Location: Moist woods; Newfoundland, southern Labrador, southeastern Manitoba to Delaware, Maryland, northern Indiana, northern Illinois, northeastern Iowa, North Carolina and Georgia mountains.
   Size: 70–80 feet (21–24m) tall; 2–3 feet (.6–.9m) in diameter.
   Wood: Very hard, heavy. Excellent fuel; throws a lot of heat; builds lasting coals.
   Animals attracted: Grouse, prairie chicken, whitetail deer, moose, cottontail rabbit, red squirrel.
   Note: Broken twigs give off a wintergreen odor.

Staminate and pistillate
flowers of the yellow birch

Bark of the yellow birch

Yellow birch with good stem
and crown characteristics

Buckeye (Hippocastanaceae)

Leaves: Opposite; palmately (shaped like an open palm) compound; coarse-toothed.

Flowers: Bell-shaped; in spring.

Fruit: 1–3 inches (2.5–7.5cm) in diameter; large leathery husk contains inedible seeds in fall.

Location: North America, southeast Europe, Asia. About one-third of the 20 species are native to the U.S.

Buckeye, Ohio (Aesculus glabra)

Leaves: 5–7 paired leaflets; 4–15 inches (10.25–37.5cm).

Bark: Dark gray, scaly.

Flowers: Yellow bells; April, May.

Fruit: Husk sports short, blunt spikes; September to October.

Location: Moist forest; West Virginia, western Pennsylvania, Iowa, southeastern Nebraska to eastern Tennessee, central Alabama and Oklahoma.

Size: 40 feet (12m) tall; 2 feet (.6m) in diameter.

Wood: Almost fireproof when green; very hard to split; good reflector fire log.

Note: Leaves and twigs have a very unpleasant odor when crushed.

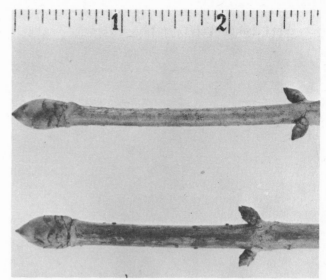

Twigs of the red buckeye (Aesculus pavia)

Flowers of the red buckeye (Aesculus pavia)

Bark of the yellow buckeye (Aesculus octandra)

Cedar, Northern White (Thuja occidentalis)
Leaves: Flat branchlets; yellow-green; aromatic; aligned vertically.
Cones: Oblong and scaly; bell-shaped; erect on branchlets.
Bark: Gray to red-brown; ridged and furrowed; fibrous.
Location: Grows in limestone soils and moist, boggy places; Nova Scotia, eastern Quebec, northern Ontario and southern Manitoba to southern New York, southern Ohio, northern Illinois, eastern Minnesota, western North Carolina and eastern Tennessee mountains.
Size: 40–50 feet (12–15m) tall; 2–3 feet (.6–.9m) in diameter.
Wood: Soft, light color; durable; good for shingles and fire-by-friction sets; outer bark good for tinder. Very decay resistant but easy to split; stumps easy to find.
Note: This tree is also known as arbor vitae, the "tree of life," for having cured the men of a Canadian expedition of scurvy. It was the first tree to be exported from U.S. to Europe. It is also known as canoe-wood, having been used by the Indians for making their boats.
Animals attracted: Deer, moose, snowshoe hare, cottontail rabbit, red squirrels, and song birds.

Pistillate flowers of the eastern red cedar (Juniperus virginiana)

Cedar, Red (Juniperus virginiana)
Needles: 1/16–3/16 (1.6–19.1mm) long; green; in pairs in four rows on four-sided branchlets; rounded.
Bark: Dry; ash gray to red-brown; fibrous.
Fruit: White to black-green berries; 1/4 inch (6.4mm) in diameter.
Cones: Green changing to blue.
Location: Grows in poor soil; best in limestone.
Size: 40–50 feet (12–15m); 1–2 feet (.3–.6m) in diameter.
Wood: At heart is rosy-brown and aromatic; light, strong, durable; used for storage chests, cabinets, pencils, fuel, and fence posts. The outer bark may be stripped and rubbed between the hands for tinder with a flint and steel set or used for combustible material with a magnifying fire set.
Animals attracted: 50 species of birds including bobwhite, sharptail grouse, pheasant, mourning dove; opossum.

Leaves and cones (berries) of the southern red cedar (Juniperus silicicola)

The southern red cedar (Juniperus silicicola)

Bark of the southern red cedar (Juniperus silicicola)

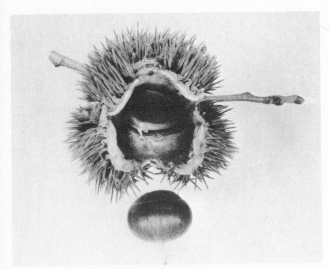

Fruit of the American chestnut tree

Chestnut (Castanea dentata)
  Leaves: Large but narrow; hairless;
     coarse-toothed.
  Bark: Dark with wide-topped shiny
     ridges when older.
  Flowers: June to August.
  Fruit: Nuts in a spiny husk; most flat on
     one side; edible; September to October.
  Location: Forest with good runoff;
     southern Maine, New York, southern
     Ontario, southern Michigan to Georgia,
     northeastern Mississippi.
  Size: Were 60–80 feet (18–24m) tall in
     prime; now are 15 feet (4.57m).
  Wood: Prized for furniture, caskets,
     fencing. Will burn green or dry; very
     decay resistant; easy to split; burns very
     slowly.
  Note: An epidemic in 1900 wiped out the
     chestnut as an important timber tree.
     Sprouts are now found only around old
     stumps and develop disease before
     maturity.

Cottonwoods (Populus)
  Leaves: Broad; coarsely toothed; alter-
     nate, long stems.
  Bark: Smooth; greenish white when
     young; dark and furrowed when older.

Fruit: Caterpillar-like catkins.
Location: Moist soil near streams; range
     across North America.
Wood: Soft, light, burns slowly when
     green with lots of noise. Decays very
     quickly. Is made into boxes, paper,
     matches.

Bark of the eastern cottonwood
(Populus deltoides)

Leaves and terminal bud of the black
cottonwood (Populus trichocarpa)

The eastern cottonwood (Populus deltoides)

Cypress, Bald (Taxodium distichum)
  Needles: ¼–⅞ inches (6.4–22.2mm)
    long, green, flat, clustered. This tree is
    not an evergreen; the needles drop in
    the winter.
  Cones: Ball-shaped; 1 inch (25.5mm) in
    diameter; woody.
  Bark: Brown; smooth but fibrous; base of
    trunk usually deeply ridged.
  Location: Found in southern swamps;
    southern New Jersey to Florida, west to
    Texas, north to southwestern Indiana,
    southern Illinois, western Kentucky
    and southeastern Missouri.
  Size: 80–120 feet (24–36m); 3–4 feet (.9–
    1.2m) in diameter.
  Wood: Valuable lumber tree for con-
    struction, posts, shingles; soft, light,
    straight grain; durable. (Related to red-
    wood.)
  Animals attracted: Songbirds and
    cranes.
  Note: Cypress "knees" are found in deep
    water. These root growths are valued as
    lamp bases and polished curios.

Bark: Smooth and dark brown to black
    in young tree; scaly and black in mature
    tree.
  Flowers: Small greenish-white flower-
    ets flanked by four petals of white, pink,
    or rose.
  Fruit: Bright red; oval; resemble a rose-
    hip but clustered.
  Location: Woodlands;   southwestern
    Maine, southern Vermont, southern
    Ontario, southern Michigan, eastern
    Kansas to Florida, eastern Texas.
  Size: 15–40 feet (4.5–12m) tall; 6–18
    inches (15.25–45.0cm) in diameter.
  Wood: Heavy, easy to split when green.
  Note: This is one of 100 species of cornus.
    They are generally found in the tem-
    perate zones and are usually shrub size.

Flowering dogwood blossoms, above and right

Dogwood, Flowering (Cornus florida)
  Leaves: Simple; opposite; 3–6 inches
    (7.5–15.25cm) long, 1½–2 inches (3.75–
    5.0cm) wide; oval and pointed; scarlet in
    fall.

Flowering dogwood in full bloom

The American elm

Bark of the American elm

Elm, American (Ulmus americana)

Leaves: Variable; smooth to rough above, hairless or hairy below; 2–6 inches (5.0–15.25cm) long.

Bark: Ridges have flat tops; mature trees are dark gray.

Flowers: March to May.

Fruit: Communion-like wafers; greenish in color.

Location: Bottomlands; Newfoundland, Nova Scotia, eastern Quebec, Saskatchewan to northern Florida, Texas.

Size: 80–100 feet (24–30m) tall; 2–5 feet (.6–1.5m) in diameter.

Wood: Easy to split; virtually fireproof.

Note: The Dutch elm disease, spread by a beetle, has to a great extent eliminated this tree. It once lined the streets of many middle-American towns. Many have had to be destroyed.

Fir, Balsam (Abies balsamea)

Needles: Flat;   0.8–1.5   inches   (2.0–3.75cm) long; blunt or notched at tip; two-ranked.

Cones: Cylindrical; purple; upright; 2–4 inches (5.0–10.25cm) long.

Bark: Young trees contain resin blisters; older tree is gray to red-brown and in scales.

Location: Bottomland and moist woods near lakes and streams; Newfoundland, Labrador, northeastern Alberta into New England, western Virginia, eastern West Virginia, northeastern Ohio, northeastern Iowa, and Minnesota. Grows low at timberline.

Size: 40–60 feet (12–18m) tall; 2–3 feet (.6–.925m) in diameter.

Wood: Soft, perishable; gum of tree used by woodsfolk as a wound plaster. Green, it is difficult to burn; seasoned, it burns fast and throws sparks; good, easy kindling in wet weather; good for fire-by-friction sets; resinous fir knots make good torches; decays very quickly.

Animals attracted: Grouse, snowshoe hare, whitetail deer, moose, and porcupine.

Leaves of the balsam fir

Balsam fir

Balsam fir cones

Hawthorns (Crataegus)

   Leaves: Alternate; toothed; lobed.
   Bark: Smooth; greenish-brown; breaks to thin scales with age.
   Flowers: Clusters of snow-white, pink, or red.
   Fruit: Apple-like but dry and mealy; red, orange; remains on tree during winter.
   Location: Eastern U.S.; Europe and Asia.
   Wood: Not commercially important.
   Animals attracted: Winter fruit provides food for birds and mammals; songbirds particularly like to hide in the thicket.
   Note: There are almost 100 species in the cooler parts of Europe and Asia and, depending on the "expert," between 100 and 1,000 in the U.S.

Leaves and cones of the Eastern hemlock (Tsuga canadensis)

Hemlock (Tusga)

   Needles: Flat; of different lengths; soft, lace-like foliage; tips droop.
   Cones: Oval to oblong; hang from branchlet tips.
   Bark: Eastern (T. canadensis): dark purple-brown, scaly; deep furrows. Car-

olina (T. caroliniana): dark red-brown; scaly; furrowed. Western (T. heterophylla): dark red-brown; scaly; furrowed. Mountain (T. mertensiana): dark purple-brown.

Location: Four species native to temperate zone of North America. Others found in Far East and Himalayas.

Size: Range from the 50-foot (15m) Carolina to the 125- to 175-foot (3.75–5.25m) Western.

Wood: The Eastern variety is used to make railroad ties; it is very knotty and throws sparks. Bark will provide a good bed of coals.

Mountain hemlock (Tsuga mertensiana) in a high alpine meadow in Oregon

(above and right)
Eastern hemlock trees (Tsuga canadensis)

Shagbark hickory

Hickories (Carya)
  Leaves: Alternate; compound; toothed.
  Flowers: Long; pointed.
  Fruit: Tri-branched catkins; edible nuts
    fall in September and October. (Pecans
    are in this family.)
  Location: Found in the Eastern U.S. pre-
    dominantely. One species in Mexico;
    two in East and Southeast Asia.
  Wood: A tough, flexible hardwood with
    wavy grain; difficult to work—use saw
    rather than ax. Used for athletic equip-
    ment, tool handles, chair backs, and
    baskets. Splits well when green. Con-
    sidered the best fuel; green makes best
    fires—most heat, burns longest, best
    coals. Used for warmth and for cooking
    and smoking meat; ashes used for
    making lye in production of homemade
    soap. Split green bark may be used as
    chewing gum!
  Animals attracted: Squirrel, opossum,
    wild turkey, duck.

Hickory, Shagbark (Carya ovata)
  Leaves: 5–7 hairless leaflets; 8–14
    inches (20.25–35.0cm) long.
  Bark: Light; very shaggy; long, loose
    strips curved at the ends.
  Fruit: Yellowish husk splits in four
    parts when ripe, revealing smooth, egg-
    shaped nuts 1½–3 inches (3.75–7.5cm)
    long.
  Location: Mature forests; southwestern
    Maine, southwestern Quebec, southern
    Ontario, central Michigan, southeast-
    ern Minnesota, southeastern Nebraska
    to northwestern Florida, eastern Texas.
  Size: 60–90 feet (18–27m) tall, 2–3 feet
    (.6–.9m) in diameter.

Shagbark hickory

Holly, American (Ilex opaca)

Leaves: Prickly, evergreen leaves, 2–4 inches (5.0–10.25cm) long; leathery, with sharp pointed tips.

Bark: Thick; gray; warty.

Flowers: May and June.

Fruit: Red, berry-like fruit appears August to June.

Location: Prefers the moist woods of lower New England (eastern Massachusetts, southeastern New York) to eastern Pennsylvania and on into southern Ohio, southeastern Missouri, Oklahoma to Florida and Texas.

Size: 50 feet (15m) tall.

Wood: Green splits easy, burns well; seasoned is hard to split but rates a bit below hickory for firing ability (gives a good, hot fire with coals). Ivory-white wood is on call for ship models and inlays.

Animals attracted: Songbirds, wild turkey, and bobwhite.

American holly

This "firecracker holly" belonging to E. Price Carpenter is shown in 1942, 30 years after he dug it up in his woods and transplanted it.

Leaves and fruit of the American holly

Bark of the American holly

Honeylocust

Leaf and fruit of the honeylocust

Honeylocust leaf

Bark of the honeylocust

Honeylocust (Gleditsia triacanthos)

Leaves: Compound; number of narrow leaflets; toothed; 6–15 inches (15.25–37.5cm) long.

Bark: Dark; scaly; stout branch thorns 3–5 inches (7.5–12.75cm) long.

Flowers: Small and greenish; cluster May through July.

Fruit: Flat, twisted pods; 8–18 inches (20.25–45.0cm) long; appear September to February; dark grayish-brown in color; called honeylocust because pods are 25 percent sugar.

Location: Moist, fertile soil; central Midwest to southern U.S.

Size: 75–80 feet (22.5–24m) tall; 2–3 feet (.6–.925m) in diameter.

Wood: Heavy and durable; one of the hardest woods; burns best green with a slow fire; good for all night. The thorns may be used for pins. Seasoned wood makes good pegs and dowels.

Animals attracted: Cows, deer, rabbit, squirrel, bobwhite.

The American hornbeam (Carpinus caroliniana)

Hornbeams (Carpinus)
  Leaves: 2–4 inches (5.0–10.25cm) long;
    1–2 inches (2.5–5.0cm) wide; double-
    toothed margin; dull green on top, yel-
    low-green underneath.
  Bark: Flat, muscular-type trunk with
    smooth gray-blue bark.
  Fruit: Seed bearing bracts (structure ap-
    pearing beneath fruit or flower) 3–6
    inches (7.5–15.25cm); bear a light
    green, leafy look in spring.
  Location: Moist, rich swamp or stream
    soil; Nova Scotia, southern Manitoba to
    Florida and Texas.
  Size: 40 feet (12m) tall; 1–2 feet (.3–.6m)
    in diameter.
  Wood: European trees related to the
    hornbeam have been used to yoke oxen.
  Animals attracted: Pheasant, bobwhite,
    grouse, deer, cottontail rabbit.

Ironwood (Carpinis caroliniana); also
  called blue beech
  Leaves: Egg-shaped; double-toothed;
    1–5 inches (2.5–12.75cm) long.
  Bark: Smooth, dark, gray; a muscular
    tree, trunk has rippled and sinewy look.
  Flowers: April.
  Fruit: Tiny nuts in three-point bracts
    appear August to October.
  Location: Bottomlands and similar
    soils; New England, southern Quebec,
    southern Ontario, eastern Minnesota to
    Florida and Texas.
  Size: 20–40 feet (6–12m) tall and 10–24
    inches (25.5–60.0cm) in diameter.
  Wood: Heavy and tough, but decays fast
    when left on the ground; one of the best
    fuels green or dry. Use a saw to cut.
  Animals attracted: Grouse, bobwhite,
    pheasant, wild turkey, gray squirrel,
    cottontail rabbit, whitetail deer.

Maple, Sugar (Acer saccharum)
  Leaves: Five-lobed; pale green beneath;
    velvety; firm; 2–10 inches (5.08–
    25.40cm) long.
  Flowers: Yellow; April to June.
  Fruit: June to September.
  Bark: Dark brown; rough, vertical
    grooves and ridges.
  Location: Mature woods in Newfound-
    land, Nova Scotia, Quebec, south-
    western Manitoba, down through
    Virginia, northern Georgia and eastern
    Texas.
  Size: 40–60 feet (12–18m) tall; 1–2 feet
    (.3–.6m) in diameter.
  Wood: A most valuable hardwood; light
    in color; wavy grained; good for carving.
    Makes a good coal fire when dry; may
    explode at start. Source of maple syrup
    and lumber for Early American fur-
    niture.

Red mulberry

Mulberry (Moraceae)
There are 1,000 species of mulberry. Related to hemp, the cordage should be suitable for temporary woodcrafts.

Mulberry, Red (Morus rubra)
Leaves: 3–5 inches (7.5–12.75cm) long; sandpaper-like; hairy underneath; marginal teeth; turn yellow in the fall.
Bark: Dark; red-brown on older trees; scaly.
Fruit: Juicy, edible fruit resembles a long blackberry; 1–1¼ inches (2.5–3cm) long; red to purple when ripe; shows June and July.

Oak, White (Quercus alba)
Leaves: 5–9 inches (12.75–22.75cm) long; contain 7–9 lobes.
Bark: White-gray with narrow, vertical blocks of scales.
Fruit: A warty, scaled cap covers more than one-third of the acorn.
Location: Can be found in either dry or moist woods in central Maine, southern Quebec, southern Ontario and Minnesota to northwestern Florida and eastern Texas.
Size: 80–100 feet (24–30m) tall; 3–4 feet (.925–1.2m) in diameter.

Wood: Very hard wood; same uses as hickory but easier to work. Burns well when green, faster when seasoned; makes excellent coals.

White oak (above and right)

Bark of the white oak

Leaves and fruit of the osage orange

Osage Orange (Maclura pomifera)

Leaves: Ovate; 3–5 inches (7.5–12.75cm) long; egg-shaped; without teeth; bright yellow in fall.

Bark: Has broad, round, scaly ridges; orange-brown; furrowed; tight; fibrous.

Fruit: Rough skin, citrus-appearing but inedible; 3–5 inches (7.5–12.75cm) in diameter; appears in October. Caution: the milky juice may cause a rash.

Location: Native to Texas, Oklahoma, and Arkansas (home of the Osage Indians). Appears in the thickets of southern New England, New York, Iowa, eastern Kansas to Georgia and the Pacific Northwest.

Size: 10–50 feet (3–15m) tall; 1–2 feet (.3–.6m) in diameter.

Wood: Yellow in color. Indians used to make bows from this tree. Boiled woodchips provide a yellow dye. Burns well when green; difficult to cut.

Pines (Pineseae)

The thirty-five species of this family found in North America are separated into two groups—the soft and hard pine trees. In the soft trees, the needles are bundled in counts of five and the cones are scaly and non-prickly. The hard pines show bundles of two to three needles in a group and have thick, woody, and prickly cones. Pines burn fast and hot; they are soft and easy to split and can be worked well with hand tools.

Ovulate flowers of the jack pine (Pinus banksiana)

Pine, Jack (Pinus banksiana); also called gray pine.

Needles: Two at a time; 1–1½ inches (2.5–3.75cm) long; stiff; dark green.

Cones: Remain on the tree for years; 1–2 inches (2.5–5.0cm) long; curved toward the tip; prickly.

Bark: Scaly; dark gray to red-brown; ragged looking.

Location: Settles for poor dry soils found in Nova Scotia, northern Quebec and the Northwest Territories, northern British Columbia, southern Manitoba, and central Alberta. In the United States: northern New England, northern New York, northwestern Indiana, northern Illinois, Minnesota.

Size: 70–80 feet (21–24m) tall; 1–1½ feet (.3–.45m) in diameter.

Wood: Easy to chop and split.

Leaves and cones of the pitch pine (Pinus rigida)

Bark of the pitch pine (Pinus rigida)

Pine, Pitch (Pinus rigida); also known as candlewood or torchpine.

Needles: Stiff; yellow-green; 3–5 inches (7.5–12.75cm) long; appear in threes.

Cones: Oval; prickly; 2–3½ inches (5.0–8.75cm) long.

Bark: Ragged looking.

Location: Prefers poor, sterile soil; Maine, eastern Ohio, to western South Carolina, northwestern Georgia and eastern Tennessee mountains. Also found in southeastern Ontario.

Size: 50–60 feet (15–18m); 1–2 feet (.3–.6m) in diameter.

Wood: Chops and splits easily; highly inflammable due to pockets of pitch in the wood.

Eastern white pine (Pinus strobus)

Pine, White (Eastern: Pinus Strobus; Western: Pinus monticola); also called soft pine.

Needles: Eastern: needles in fives; 3–5 inches (7.5–12.75cm) long; soft and flexible; stay on tree 1–2 years; white on two surfaces of the needle provide the name.

Cones: Eastern: 4–8 inches (10.25–
20.25cm) long. Western: curved; 5–15
inches (12.75–37.5cm) long; eight to a
set.

Bark: Eastern is smooth and gray when
young; rectangular blocks appear on
older trees.

Location: Eastern: moist, sandy soil of
the uplands; Newfoundland, central
Ontario, and southwestern Manitoba to
eastern Maryland, western North Carolina, northern Georgia, eastern Tennessee and northeastern Iowa.

Size: Eastern: 75–100 feet (22.5–30m)
tall; 2–4 feet (.6–1.2m) in diameter.

Wood: Moderately resistant to decay;
does not burn well even when split; sea-
soning helps.

Great Basin sage

Sagebrush (Artemisia tridentata)

Leaves: 1½ inches (3.75cm) long; alternate; wedge-shaped and toothed at the
outward end.

Flowers: Drab brown; long and in narrow clusters.

Location: A gnarled shrub common to
the western states; desert country.

Note: Its foliage may be used as shelter
material.

Spruce (Picea)

Needles: Short, stiff, sharp; grow all
over the twig.

Cones: Brown and woody when mature;
hang down rather than erect.

Bark: Rough and dark.

Location: Receptive to the moist soil and
cooler temperatures of the Northern
Hemisphere. Found north to the
tundra.

Wood: In Europe some spruces are
tapped for turpentine; others provide
medicinal compounds. Inner bark can
be dried, ground, and added to flour to
extend it. Beer is made by boiling the
fermented needles and sticks of the red
and black spruce with honey. Decays
quickly; easy to split.

Note: Colloquialism "spruced up" refers
to this tree's immaculate appearance.

Englemann spruce

Spruce, Englemann (Picea englemannii)
Needles: Plump and prickly.
Cones: 1–2½ inches (2.54–6.25cm) long; light red-brown with ragged edges.
Bark: Scaly; purple to red-brown.
Location: At high elevation in Rockies.
Size: 100–125 feet (30–37.5m) tall; 1–3 feet (.3–.9m) in diameter.
Wood: A timber industry tree.

Spruce, Norway (Pinea abies)
Needles: Stiff; dark green; flat to tri-angular.
Cones: Brown;   4–7   inches   (10.16–17.78cm) long.
Bark: Reddish-brown.
Location: Europe and the U.S.
Size: 125 feet (37.5m) tall; 2 feet (.6m) in diameter.

Norway spruce leaves and cone

Spruce, White (Picea glauca)
Needles: Similar to the black spruce; 1 inch (2.54cm) long; crowded on the upper side of the branch.
Cones: 1–2½ inches (2.54–6.25cm) long; thin and woody, but flexible.
Bark: Outer bark is ash brown; inner is silver when cut.

Location: Prefers streams and lake lo-cales and the upland soils of Newfound-land, Labrador, Alaska to Maine; also northwestern Massachusetts, northern New York, Michigan, Minnesota, western South Dakota and Wyoming. (The black spruce (P. mariana) prefers the swamps.)
Size: 75 feet (22.5m) tall; 2 feet (.6m) in diameter.
Wood: Also known as pasture, swamp or skunk spruce, this tree emits an un-pleasant odor, but it makes good kind-ling.

White spruce

A 40- to 50-year-old stand of
American sycamore trees

Sycamore, American (Platanus occidentalis)
  Leaves: Alternate; 3–5 lobes; edged with
    good-size teeth; almost hairless; 4–8
    inches (10.5–20.25cm) wide.
  Bark: Peels irregularly to create a mot-
    tled brown exterior effect; yellow or
    white underneath.
  Flowers: April to June.
  Fruit: Multiple "button balls" made up
    of many-winged seeds which break
    apart releasing the ripe seeds to the
    wind. These balls may often be seen
    through the winter months.
  Location: Found along the banks of
    streams and in the rich bottom lands of
southwestern Maine, New York,
southern Ontario, central Michigan,
Iowa and eastern Nebraska to north-
western Florida and central Texas. Of
the six species, three are native to the
U.S.; others appear in Mexico, Central
America, Southwest Asia, and south-
eastern Europe.
  Size: 100 feet (30m) tall; 3–10 feet (.925–
    3.0m) in diameter.
  Wood: Hard; coarse-grained; makes
    good boxes, furniture, and butcher's
    blocks.
  Note: The sycamore is old at 600.

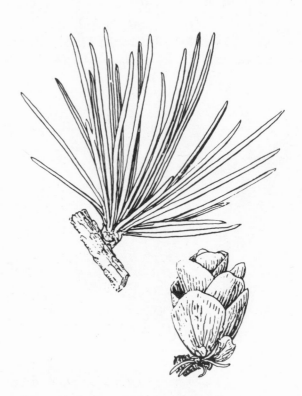

Leaves and cone of the tamarack

Tamarack (Larix laricina); also called
  American larch.
  Needles: To 1 inch (2.5cm) long; many
    on short spurs.
  Cones: ½–¾ inch (1.25–1.75cm) long.

Bark: Dark; thin; scaly; gray to reddish-
brown.

Location: Prefers bog soils and wooded
swamps. Found in Newfoundland, Labrador, Alaska to northern New Jersey,
northern Maryland, northern West Virginia, northeastern Illinois, Minnesota,
and northwestern British Columbia.

Size: 40–80 feet (12–24m); 1–2 feet (.3–
.6m) in diameter.

Wood: Easy to work with green or dry;
burns best dry; provides intense (but
short-lived) heat—good for cooking.

Animals attracted: Ruffed grouse, snowshoe hare, red squirrel, deer, and porcupine.

Tamarack

Tuliptree (Liriodendron tulipifera)

Leaves: Four-point leaves; 6–10 inches
(15.24–25.40cm) long; hairless twigs
and leaves. Gives off spicy scent when
crushed.

Bark: Light gray; white in grooves.

Flowers: Large and like namesake;
orange and green; blooms May and
June.

Fruit: Slim; winged; white; of a cone-
like appearance; 3 inches (7.5cm) long.
Appears September to November.

Location: Thrives in the fertile woods of
·Massachusetts, southern Vermont,
southern Ontario, southern Michigan,
southern Illinois, down to central Florida, Louisiana and eastern Arkansas.

Size: 50–100 feet (15–30m) tall; 2–6 feet
(.6–1.75m) in diameter.

Wood: Straight grained; fine; soft and
resists splitting; easy to work. Makes
furniture, shingles, boats, tools, boxes,
toys, and fuel.

Pistillate flowers of the black walnut

Walnut, Black (Juglans nigra)

Leaves: 12–24 inches (.3–.6m) long; contain 15–23 leaflets; smooth above, hairy
below; spicy when crushed.

Bark: Dark brown to black; furrowed.

Flowers: April to June.

Fruit: October and November; spherical

A bumper crop of black walnuts

1½–2 inches (3.75–5.0cm). Thick yellow-green husk covers a woody, grooved, edible nut.
Location: Western Massachusetts, southern Ontario, southern Minnesota, southeastern South Dakota to northwestern Florida, eastern Texas and western Oklahoma.
Size: 70–100 feet (21–30m) tall; 2–3 feet (.6–.9m) in diameter.
Wood: Hard, heavy, strong, and durable; splits easily; works well; slow burning firewood.
Animals attracted: Squirrels, mice, deer.

Note: The nut husk provides a dark brown dye when boiled.

Walnut, English (Juglans regia); also known as Circassian walnut.
Leaves 8–16 inches (20.32–40.0cm) long; 7–9 leaflets.
Fruit: Nut inside a thin-shelled, round, and ridged sphere contained within a green, smooth husk 1½–2 inches (3.75–5.08cm) in diameter.
Location: Native to southeastern Europe, India, China. Provides the basis of commercial walnut production in the U.S.
Size: 70 feet (21m) tall; 3 feet (.925m) in diameter.

Willow (Salix)
There are 325 species (including these poplars and aspens) in this family. They are abundant in the Northern Hemisphere with 100 in North America alone. Forty of them are tree size. Their preference is for dense thickets near water. This has been capitalized on by using the willow to retard streambed erosion. The twigs of the willow are flexible and make good basketry material.

Willow, Basket (Salix viminalis)
Leaves: 2½–3½ inches (6.25–8.75cm) long; smooth and dark green above, silk white and finely haired below.
Flowers: April through May.
Location: Introduced from Europe to the East Coast, it is still common there but is also found from Wisconsin to Virginia, West Virginia, Ohio, and Iowa. Like all willows, it is partial to damp soil.
Wood: Light; grows straight and fast; younger are white and hard; older are yellow, soft, and easier to work. Decays very quickly.

Witch-Hazel (Hamamelis virginiana)

Leaves: Alternate; 4–6 inches (10.25–15.25cm) long, 2–3 inches (5.0–7.5cm) wide with deep teeth. Leaves are dull green on top and light underneath.

Bark: Smooth or rough in patches; has cross striping.

Flowers: September through November; four narrow petals showing fall and winter.

Fruit: August through October; two-peaked wood capsule splits, sending shiny black seeds up to 20 feet (6.0m) in distance when open.

Location: Woods; near streams; in moist soils; Nova Scotia, southern Ontario, central Michigan, southeastern Minnesota to central Florida, eastern Texas.

Size: To 30 feet (9m) tall; 12 inches (.3m) in diameter.

Wood: Decay resistant.

Animals attracted: Pheasant, bobwhite, ruffed grouse, whitetail deer, cottontail rabbit, and beaver.

Leaves of the witch-hazel

Fruit of the witch-hazel

Yucca (Yucca)

Leaves: Light to dark green; stiff and sword-like; thick at base and sharply pointed at tip; 6–10 inches (15.25–25.5cm) long; finely toothed; clustered at the ends of thick branches.

Flowers: Cup-shaped and open at night; white, streaked with green or purple; in six segments.

Fruit: Oval to oblong; flat, black seeds.

Location: A desert plant, the yucca occurs only in the Western Hemisphere.

Size:15–30 feet (4.5–9m); 1–3 feet (.3–.9m) in diameter.

Wood Selection

Once you've achieved a nodding acquaintance with the trees in your locale, you will come to the next crucial step—that of the selection of the proper wood for the job at hand. For instance, to feed the flame for warmth and cooking you will need dry, brittle wood, that which has lost its bark and does not feel cold. To find dry wood in the rain, poke under the branches of a dense bush or take the lowest and dead pine boughs. Even sticks found lying in an open downpour will burn. If you cut away the wet layer, the center will be dry.

To select the proper wood, you should know the bark as well as the leaf structure of the tree so you can recognize the tree in the winter and readily identify a fallen tree on the forest floor. And, you need to know what each can and cannot do. For instance, the soft woods are quick to fire and give off with a short, light, and easy flame. So, they make good kindling. For better burning, rely on:

- Jack pine
- Buckeye
- Chestnut
- Largetooth aspen
- Cottonwood
- Quaking aspen
- Red cedar
- Soft maple

By far, the best and lasting firewoods are:

- Apple
- White ash
- Beech
- Black, yellow, and white birch
- Dogwood
- Hickory
- Holly
- Hornbeam

- Ironwood
- Locust
- Sugar maple
- Mulberry
- White oak (a steady burner)
- Yellow pine (leaves coals)
- Tamarack

Before the bonfire comes the kindling. The barks of cedar, hemlock, and birch set themselves above others as fire starters. In fact, birch bark will start a fire with only a sliver, and that sliver may be dripping wet! (You can find these small pieces as coils at the bottom of a shedding tree.) Dry twigs, tiny-to-one-half-pencil size which snap when you walk on them, are good by the handful.

Other characteristics of certain kinds of wood lend themselves to the woodcraft arts. You'll want to know just which woods are pliable, will bend easily to form baskets and other flexible material. Those pliable woods are:

- Basswood
- Hackberry
- Redbud
- Witch-hazel
- Elm
- Bigbud hickory
- Yellow poplar

Those woods which ease the making of wood objects by virtue of their simplicity to split are:

- Arbor vitae (northern white cedar)
- Basswood
- Cedar
- Chestnut
- Green slippery elm
- Soft pine
- Spruce

- Ash
- Green beech
- White birch
- Green black birch
- Green dogwood
- Balsam fir
- White, red and black oak

This is only a sampling of the 800 kinds of trees in the United States alone. To know them all, you must begin with a few, and to know those few well, you need to live among them and use them well, with respect and proper care.

Wood Preparation

Wood may be used as it is found, or it may be altered to fit the job. It may seem simple to take a log, fit the saw to it, and go. Or it may not appear to take more than a dead-eye and a good swing to make kindling out of timber. But there's a bit more to it than that—including safety.

The kindling sticks may take nothing more than a sharp crack over a raised knee, but don't try it with more than pencil size. A slightly larger piece of wood may be grooved on either side with your knife and struck sharply on a convenient log or large rock at the notches.

The next size larger will probably require your hatchet or ax. Lean the short log up against a fallen tree trunk. Stand to the side and angle your blow to drive the cut end down so it won't fly up and strike you, and so that any miscalculated blow won't send your ax into the dirt causing it to dull.

Log Splitting: To split that same size log lengthwise, again lean the log against a fallen trunk, but this time stand on the opposite side of the tree trunk and swing with a firm blow. You may also set fireplace-length

Splitting a log

logs on end and swing your ax into the up-turned end twisting slightly on contact to pry the wood open. If there are naturally occurring splits, aim for these. Remember, take the easiest route. The code of the seasoned forester: "If it's easy, it's right!"

Splitting a full length log is a bit more work. Again, look for a natural break line visible at the ends of the log. Stand facing down the log's length. Using two axes, drive the first in on the "fault line." Then turn to face the opposite direction and drive the second ax into the crack made by the first but a bit farther down the log. Alternate this ax head-to-ax head procedure for the length of the log. (If wedges are needed, make them out of apple or ironwood; see Chapter 1).

The final cut in splitting a full-length log

To divide a full length log into short pieces, another process is used. Bracing the fallen tree trunk with one foot, hold the ax with both hands and chop a wedge-shaped notch out of one side. (Chopping at an angle eases the work.) The notch should be as wide (side-to-side) as the log is deep. Step down and mark the edges of the notch correspondingly on the other side and chop it out. With the major girth of the log removed you will be able to sever it with a few passes at the narrowed joint.

Following a hew line, a fallen log is flattened on one side.

Hewing: You may want to leave that full-length log as is and make a camp "sofa" out of it. To flatten the giant on one side you will first need a hew line made of string cut the length of the log. Set a notch at either end of the log, equidistant from the top, and attach the string in the notches. Blacken the string with charcoal and, pulling it back at the middle, snap it sharply against the side of the log. Repeat this procedure on the opposite side. An even, black line will be left which will guide the depth of the series of notches to be made along the top length of the log. Chop the wood out between the notches and your seat is completed.

Curing: Not all available wood is the prime, dry kind best suited for making the gadgets and comforts illustrated later in this book. But green wood may be quick-cured to serve the purpose. Roasting green wood in the hot ashes of the fire, or over it, will make it soft and pliable. This heated wood may even be straightened by hanging it from an overhead limb with a weight at the bottom. The wood will stiffen when cooled.

Small pieces of wood may be quick-cured by boiling them in water for 24 hours to draw out the sap. They are ready when all of the water has evaporated from the curing pot. Small pieces may also be dried beside the fire overnight. Take care that they do not get hot enough to warp or char, however. To season large logs you can build a raised rack 3–4 feet (90–120cm) off the ground and stack logs tepee-style around it. Build a little fire or fires inside the structure. Keep it going for as long as a week and keep an eye on it so it does not go out or set the drying logs ablaze. The logs may be turned several times to quicken the drying.

It is not that there is a mystery to wood-crafting. But, like everything else there is a right and a wrong way to do things. The simple art of removing a branch from a log is an example. Rather than striking the branch at the inside of its connection with the tree and having to take a second step to even the end and remove the extra bark, simply strike the joint in the direction the branch normally grows. The separation will be clean and require no added work.

Making Pegs and Hooks: Finally, as in all human activity, it is the little things that count. It is the whittling of pegs, poles, and hooks which hold tarp and timber together. A good supply of wood pegs will make roughing it a lot easier.

Pegs and forks are basically the same: they are simple and fit a variety of jobs. To whittle a peg, select a straight and solid branch, cut it into the lengths and number of pegs needed for a job. For ease in pounding, bevel one end of each length and sharpen the other to a point. The end must be pointed or the peg will drive into the ground at an angle and not hold. And it must be straight or the striking blow will be deflected and ineffective.

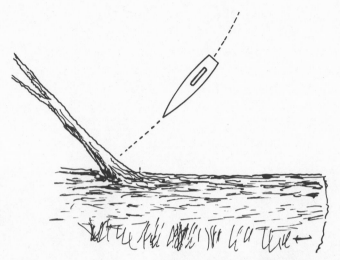

De-limbing a fallen tree

A forked stick, used for propping up cooking "cranes" and for other homespun duties, also must be made from a straight stick with the fork coming out at an angle from the side, *not* the top, of the main branch. To pound a "Y" fork is almost impossible without splitting the peg; nor can a bent fork be pounded straight into the ground. (To drive a stake into the ground you may use a large stone held in two hands. Again, let the weight of this tool do the work.)

It is not what you take with you; it is what you do with what you find that makes you a wilderness woodcrafter. Making do is an old world custom that deserves revival. These few basics should be all you need to create a myriad of tools and artifacts to set up life in the wilderness overnight, over a long weekend, or even for the rest of your days.

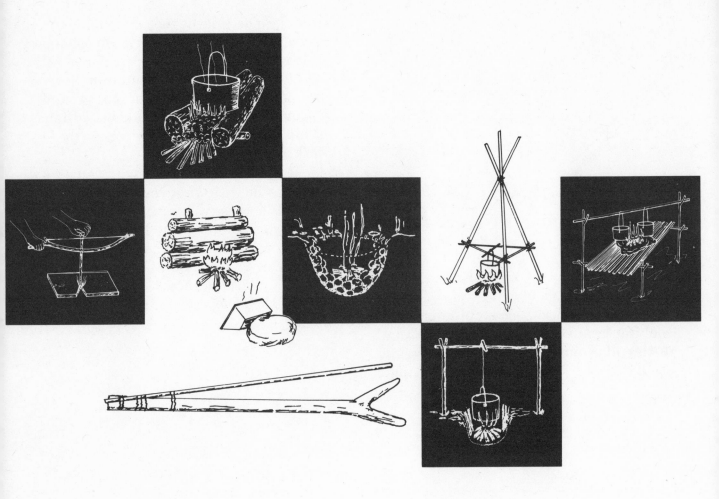

3

Fire

There is a tribe of fast disappearing primitives which carries its fire from one nomadic site to another. Perhaps it is partly a spiritual habit and partly because it is difficult to find dry kindling in the rain-forest. Fortunately, fire is one item you do not need to find room for in the corner of your pack.

If you are camping—in a national or state park or forest—it is likely that a site will be designated or will have been used before for making a fire. If so, use it. If not, choose your site carefully, keep it as small as possible, and when you are through, cover its traces, returning the site to its pre-fire condition. As a matter of fact, it is becoming common for parks in many areas to forbid fire-building, because of forest fire danger or ecological damage.

Your fire site should be on clear earth, free of underbrush and flammable branches. Make sure you are not building on punky, humus soil (that which contains rotting wood and other vegetation, usually soft to the step). The heat can be retained in such ground long after you leave and can spread,

flaming up yards away and days later. The best site is on sand, rock, or a combination of the two. Build on the firmest ground you can find, cleared of dead vegetation—not ravaged—for a diameter of 6 feet. Don't place your campfire at the foot of a tree, dead or alive, or even at the base of a stump. It doesn't take much time to plan a fire. First, it should be built to serve a variety of purposes—for cooking and day and nighttime warmth, to touch on two. Inexperienced campers tend to build big, blazing fires which char the soles of sneakers as well as the meat and marshmallows. Big is not better. Your fire does not have to win any prizes; it's just another tool.

Starting with split wood, because it burns the easiest, stack it so that air will circulate through as well as around the fire, providing its prime ingredient, oxygen. You may build a fast fire to start, using dry tinder to give a quick, hot flame which will catch the full and slower-to-burn logs later. Planning also includes having enough wood for the project. If you keep a supply on hand, your fire won't burn down while you are out chopping more; the hurry might cause you to be careless, too.

Given forethought, you have probably brought your own matches—2½ inches (6.25cm) long—which will light on the seat of your pants. And they are keeping dry in a plastic tube or a 12–20 gauge fired shotgun shell. The tip of each may have been dipped in paraffin or nailpolish for added protection against moisture. Extras may be stored in the bored buttplate of a rifle, wooden back-pack frame, moneybelt, or knife sharpening kit in your pocket. Such preparation will save a lot of time and trouble. But, if you skipped out of town with only your wit and wisdom and you are open to the challenge of the Indian way, there is still a means to warmth and hot food.

Wilderness Fire Kits

The fire drill set is easy to make and easy to use. To begin with, look for dead, softwood trees around the campsite. In the East, forage for balsam, cedar, basswood, willow, tamarack, and American or slippery elm. In the South, good woods for this project are cypress, cottonwood, and willows. In the Southwest, there's yucca; and in the West, the cottonwood, willows, and red cedar will do fine.

Split a log, making a drill "bit" stick roughly octagonal, 12 inches (.3m) long, ¾ inch (1.75cm) in diameter, pointed at one end and beveled at the other. The fireboard, made of the same wood, is shaped 1 inch (2.5cm) thick, 12–15 inches (30–37.5cm) long, and 3 inches (7.5cm) wide. It is notched with an old-fashioned keyhole-shaped notch ⅜ of an inch (1cm) from the edge.

To fashion the bow, find a curved hardwood stick about 27 inches (68cm) long and

with a short branch stub on one end. A leather thong, shoelace or the twisted inner bark of a tree may be used as the bow "string." Attach the thong to either end of the bow and twist it around the drill stick a couple of times. For those who are not in a rush and would like to try a hand at Indian fire making, a bow may also be made using the sapling of an ash or maple. Season the wood by soaking it for 24 hours and then immersing it in boiling water. Tie a strong cord ⅛–¼ of an inch (3–6.5mm) wide to either end of the sapling, bending it slightly. Retie it every few hours to increase the bend until there are 3–5 inches (7.5–12.5cm) from the center of the bow to the cord. (Remember, never use saplings on public land.)

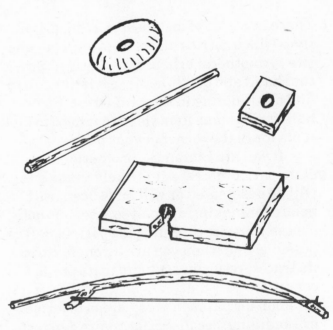

The do-it-yourself fire drill kit

The socket with which you will hold the drill stick steady at the top is made of a hardwood burl or other rounded, half-spherical piece of wood. (A glass percolator top from home is a good substitute.) In the center of the flat side you will bore a hole large enough to fit the head of the drill stick. Lubricate the hole with clay mud, grease, or crushed oily leaves so the drill will move smoothly. Most plant leaves contain oil cells. For drill lubrication take the young and tender new branchlet leaves and crush and place them between socket and drill stick.

Compose a nest of tinder. The best is made of red cedar bark, but lacking that you may use shredded chestnut, slippery elm, or cottonwood—any dry, inflammable wood shavings. Other finds that work as tinder are dry moss, dry leaves, shredded rope and twine, and field-mice nests.

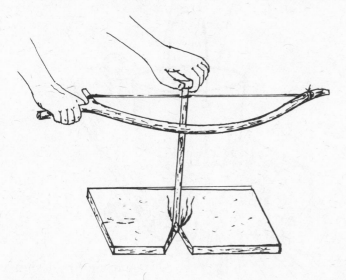

The original "fire drill" in use

Holding the drill firmly to the notch of the fireboard with the left hand, saw back and forth gently with the bow in the right hand. As the wifts of smoke show at the base, speed up the sawing. When smoke begins to rise steadily and the notch starts to blacken, remove the drill and bow, tap the board so the spark from the notch falls into the prepared tinder, and blow it gently into flame.

The key points to remember in using the fire drill set properly are:

1. Hold the drill board firmly.
2. Keep the drill steady.
3. Use long, even, full-length strokes.
4. Press down hard.
5. Lift the drill carefully so as not scatter the powder and disperse the spark.

The pump drill illustrated and explained in Chapter 1 also is good for fire making. Merely attach a blunt wooden point to the bottom end of the drill shaft and use as directed with a notched piece of softwood.

If tinder as mentioned is not available, you may prepare a prayer or fuzz stick to give your fire a start. Taking a stick of dry softwood about 1 foot (.3m) long and 1 inch (2.5 cm) thick, whittle a point on one end. Carefully carve long, thin shavings up the stick leaving them attached. You will need to press hard and deep with the knife. Push the pointed end of the fuzz stick into the ground at your fire site and build a pyramid of other kindling sticks around it.

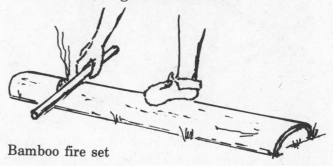

Bamboo fire set

For woodcrafters in warmer climates, bamboo and the art of the aborigines should do to start the camp's fire. Many native tribes around the world use a one-half lengthwise slice of dry bamboo as their fireboard. The bamboo length is grooved crosswise near one end, and inside the tissue below the groove is splintered to form tinder. Another piece of bamboo, cut sharp on one side, is used as the saw. Holding the bamboo fireboard down with your knee, bear down and saw slowly back and forth in the groove with the sharpened bamboo. Speed up your sawing motion. The dry powder falling on the tinder below will ignite it. Then you simply turn the bamboo over and fan the flame or blow gently to keep it alight.

Finally, yet another fire igniter is the drill set in simplified form. The hand drill and fireboard are made just as though for the full set. The drilling action is created by spinning the drill between the palms of the hands starting at the top and stroking 5–6 times back and forth. When your hands have reached the bottom, begin again at the top.

Now that the kindling has ignited, what is the architecture for the full fire?

The housing of the Indian and the settler suggest this fire arrangement. The shape of a tepee, it has a wigwam fire under a log cabin top structure.

A fire structure of crisscrossed logs is the camper's fundamental fire. It is built with the tinder on the ground covered with a 6-inch (15.25cm) wigwam. Four poles, 2 inches (5cm) thick and a foot (.3m) long, form the sides of the base. The crisscrossed

layers are made up of ¼–½ inch (6.5–12.5mm) diameter hardwood sticks built up to 10–12 inches (25.5–30.0cm) high. Over this the stew pot or soup kettle is hung.

Cooking Fire

A good fire is to a camp cook what gourmet gadgets are to a chef. It makes a difference how the meal tastes whether it is green-stick broiled hotdogs or flaming crepes. The best cooking fire—a flame for boiling and coals for broiling—is one built so the cook can get close enough to work.

A basic fire design for one-pot cooking

This second fire design makes use of two side logs set parallel to one another and angled together slightly, the wide end windward. A tinder of dry or green twigs and sticks is set between the logs. A damper stick raises one of the side logs slightly for ventilation. The pot is set on the logs over the fire.

This basic design forms the support for a fireplace made to accommodate three or four

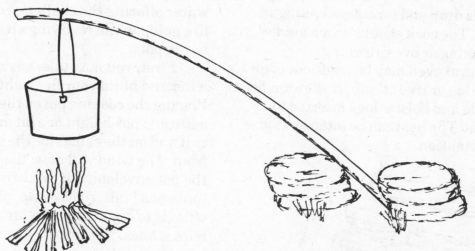

One step cooking; with rocks

cooking pots and pans in a row. A softwood tinder wigwam is flanked by the fire logs of the same size as previously used. Across the logs, the camp cook lays a grid of criss-crossed green branches along the length of the logs or as wide as is necessary to support the number of cooking pots.

When wood is scarce but stones are plenty use a marriage of both. Avoiding limestone, which pops when hot, form a fire design as above but using stones instead of the side logs. The pot may be supported with a log pole and a pot hook. The latter is a long pole of non-flammable wood which has a fork at one end to hold a pot over the fire. At the other end, the staff is securely braced on a rock and held down by another.

What we've been building so far have been fried-egg-and-hot-tea fires. Other foods take another touch or two. A stew fire, for instance, must be slow, steady, and last a long time. It is best set underground for even cooking. A hole is dug 1 foot (.3m) wide and 6 inches (20.25cm) deep with perpendicular sides. It should be 4–5 inches (10–13cm) larger around than the stewpot. The hole is lined with split hardwood logs—sugar maple, white oak, hickory, beech, yellow birch, sycamore, or persimmon—and a tepee bed of

green sticks made in the bottom. The stew pot is suspended over the hole until the flames die down, then lowered into it to slow-cook. Fuel may be added as needed along the sides.

A stew pot fire

A baking fire is of another sort, but familiar. The fundamental two-log fire is laid with a third log set nearby as though for the base of a triangle. This log is boosted up on stumps or stones and against it rests the wrought iron skillet containing bread or biscuit dough. Facing the fire, the dough rises as the coals drop and continues baking in their heat. The cook should watch out for uneven baking or overbrowning.

A natural oven may be made out of an old hollow log or tree stump. A wigwam fire is set inside and bolster logs inserted to hold the pot. The heat can be intense, so give it lots of attention.

Bread baking in a fire's reflection

The best baking fire is the reflector fire—which also provides considerable heat for cold bodies at night—and provides protection for flames against a prevailing breeze. Green logs 4–5 feet (1.21–1.5m) long are sunk into the ground at an angle. Two shorter brace logs are set evenly and a bit forward of the large posts. Between these are stacked 4 foot (1.2m) long and 6–8 inch (15.0–20.0cm) in diameter green logs. The wigwam, or other basic campfire, is set in front of the reflector. A pot may be hung from forked sticks to either side, and of course, the bread goes on baking propped at an angle on its booster log nearby. Later, you may sleep in comfort in a tent open to the reflector fire, the night's horizontal radiator.

All cooks have special occasion meals. The camper-cook is no exception. His or her special occasion, however, may be more of the special effects kind—high wind or high water offering the challenge of keeping the fire going while worrying about the goodies in the pots.

First, you may take advantage of the wind and build your fire right in its face. Placing the cooking pot on the ground, build a fire just pot-height or a bit more right next to it and on the same side the wind is coming from. The wind will blow the flames around the pot enveloping it and bringing its contents to a boil. Another way to weather the wind is to dig a pit at the fire site and line it with stones. The fire may be made at the bottom of the pit and stay lit despite the blow at ground level.

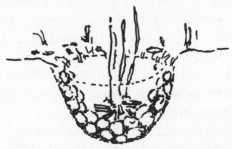

A windy day pit fire

Keeping the kettle going in a rainy wood or swamp situation is a bit trickier. If you have only puddles to contend with, simply lay two or three green logs side by side and build a small crisscross fire on top. But if the water is higher than your mocassin tops, the four-legged fire might be the only thing saving you from cold beans. Select four strong, straight branches long enough to raise your fire platform several inches above the waterline. The branches set at two diagonal corners ideally should be longer than the other two and have two forks, one at the top and one at the level you want to build the platform. Set the logs in a square, and rest or lash the framing sticks between them. Across these sticks rest evenly shaped green branches, and in an area big enough to build a fire, cover the platform with mud. A pole passed between the upper forks of the diagonal posts forms a pot holder for several pots to cook over your swamp fire at once.

varied as the imagination and necessity dictate. The Chippewa used an A-frame kitchen affair using three multi-forked branches lashed at the top in tepee fashion. About two-thirds of the way down, sticks were lashed between the mainstays to form a triangle and another branch set between two of the sides to hold the pot.

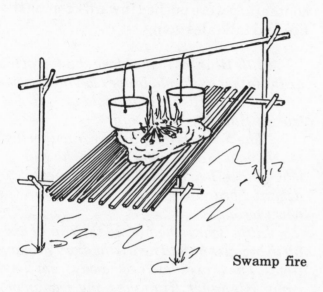

Swamp fire

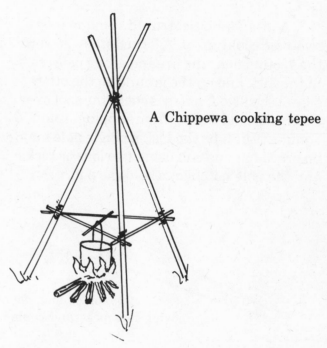

A Chippewa cooking tepee

A backlog fire is another fundamental campfire. Built of parallel logs with a backlog set to form three sides of a square, it provides cooking room for a two-course meal. A long branch is braced by a small log or rock on the outside of the backlog and rests across it. The pot hangs over a wigwam fire. Crossing the side logs are two log rests under which coals glow. A skillet with a slow cooking food rests overtop.

The structure over the fire may be as

Another cooking device can be constructed to give you a range of heats by regulating the distance the pot hangs above the

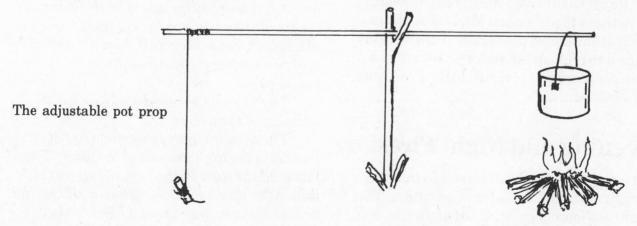

The adjustable pot prop

fire. A forked branch is whittled sharp at one end, set into the ground and wedged several feet from the fire. A long pole with a fork at the pot end rests in the fork of the branch and is held parallel to the ground, with a peg and cord at the butt end. By wrapping or unwrapping the cord around the pole, the cooking pot is raised or lowered, respectively.

A less sophisticated old standby is the two-pole cooking set. A forked stake is set in the ground near the fire and a long pole rests in the fork and on the ground on the other side of the fire. A notch is cut in the spot over the fire to hold the pot from slipping. And the simplest shall be the last: a single pole may be braced at one end using two logs or rocks and the pole notched to hold the pot.

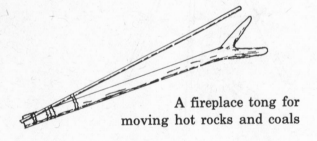

A fireplace tong for
moving hot rocks and coals

Tongs: A simple stick device can make your fire tending a bit more professional. Pick up a wide forked green stick with a long handle and a straight stick of equal length. Place them together and bind them with a thong at the end of the handle. This tool may be used to pick up hot rocks for cooking or move coals around to regulate the fire's heat and direction.

Evening and Night Fires

With dinner cooked and stories to tell, the campfire still is the center of attention. The starfire, a loosely constructed night fire, was a favored Indian fire for ancestral tales and boasts of accomplishments. A wigwam fire at the center, dry logs were set to radiate from the fire in all directions like the gleam of a star. As these branches burned in the center they were pushed inward keeping the fire and tall tales going.

Little Bear sat in the black shadow of his grandfather as the old brave read the signs in the council fire ashes and retold the old stories. Stalking Wind said:

"The fire bids well. The year will bring much meat to our lodges. It is as the year when Little Bear came. Then the ashes told of deer and bear and buffalo. The ashes are never wrong."

Little Bear remembered the year of his birth because he had heard the story so many times. The braves had been away from the camp. His father, Running Long, was among them.

The shade was dappled with sunlight. Running Long was spotted with shade and sun and the juice of plants to look like shadows. In his mind he was a fawn seeing all around him for the first time, aware of every danger, his body alternately taut and relaxed as he watched the deer graze. Other braves were shadows in the woods around him. They all watched the deer.

The woods moved under the foot of a new brave, a young boy the age of Little Bear now, on his first hunting party. Suddenly, the shadows became men and the deer started and ran swifter than the shadows and were lost to them.

The boy was shamed and learned the stillness of the woods.

The hunting party moved on out of the trees into the high grasses of the plain. They followed the dust in the sun, the sign of buffalo. After days of watching and walking, the braves came to the edge of a herd. They circled it away from the wind and became as shoots of tall grass to fool the buffalo. They watched and readied their bows. They chanted silent words to the eagle that the feathers on their arrows might be as swift and silent as he. They waited . . . too long. The wind changed and the buffalo sensed the men among the grasses and were gone in thunder and dust that shut out the sun for a day. The braves walked on to a new wood.

That night around the fire that burned to cook the small hare the youngest brave had caught, the hunting party told the tales of successful hunts and renewed their patience of stone. Each brave recounted his first kill, the happiness of his family through the months their bellies were full, the warmth of the skins of their fallen prey. The starfire shone in the faces of the braves. Tomorrow they would be sucessful and return to their homes.

Running Long awoke to the smell of bear, the rancid, oily scent that had made his hair sharpen on the back of his neck. The others caught the scent at the edge of dawn dreams and came back. The hunt began early that day.

The signs were clear—broken branches and droppings that steamed in the cold morning air. The braves followed the lucky black bear, the game that would erase the failures of the days before and the threat of hunger.

Running Long led the braves among the trees. He knew the wood, having hunted there with his father, and he knew where the bear was going. A stream with many fish ran through the wood, and the bear was going to eat.

The trees thinned slightly. Running Long motioned the others to spread out along the stream. Some moved far away to each side, crossed the stream and doubled back on the other side.

The bear stood alone in the clear stream watching the stones and the shadows of leaves, moving quickly only when the water streaked silver with the scales of a fish. He had come at a good time. There was much to eat.

Engrossed as he was, he did not hear or see the braves as they crept upon him. The wind brought the smell of men to him and he raised up startled, angry, only afraid at the last moment when the arrows came, and he fell among the stones and leaves and silver streaks.

The braves shouted once and began immediately to recount the kill. It was the beginning of the story that Little Bear was to hear many times. The bear was dressed and prepared for the return to camp. Running Long was granted the skin for his new lodge.

"May the seeds of braves be planted under this skin," the others said in joke and in blessing. When they returned, Little Bear, his first son, had been born.

The bear was the first of much game to be killed that year. The buffalo and the deer seemed to follow the hunting parties and require no stalking. It was from the cooking and council fires of that year that Stalking Wind had learned to read the coals and ashes. This night he had read another year, the coming year, a year of plenty for the people. It would be Little Bear's first year as a brave. He believed the prophecy of the ashes and looked forward to telling his first tale of a successful hunt to braves and chiefs gathered around future fires.

The day starts early when you are living outdoors, and sleep comes on early, too. That very fire that has cooked the evening meal and has been the center stage for story telling now changes function again to become warmth for the night. The fastest and easiest way to create a night fire is to rake the coals into a center pile, bank the edges with dirt or ashes and put large logs close together on top. If possible, construct a log reflector wall to direct the heat into the shelter area.

When the wind is steady in one direction, you may try a "caterpillar" fire. With a wigwam fire at one end, run a log windward with one end in the fire and the sides and middle supported by green branches. Set the next log at the end and, overlapping the first, repeat the support procedure. The fire will gradually burn up the logs keeping your campsite warm through the night.

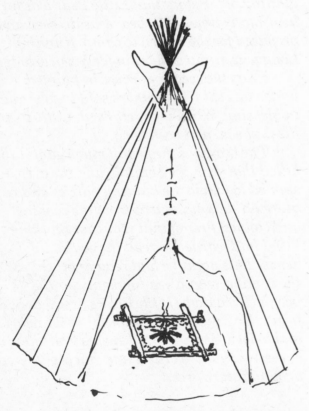

How to keep your wigwam warm

Another warm and lasting fire is composed of three or four logs, 3–5 feet (.925–1.5m) long, laid down in a square and layered once or twice. A pyramid fire is set *on the top* to start. As the coals fall from the

top they ignite the logs below and keep the fire going through the night with heat radiating all around.

The last fire to keep your wigwam warm is just that, a fire site designed to fit in the center of a tepee. A 3–4 inch (7.5–10.25cm) deep square pit is dug just under the tepee's smoke hole. Appropriately sized logs are notched, laid within the square and staked at the corners to hold them firm. Stones are laid in lining the logs and the fire is set within the framework for the night. Just don't try this inside an ordinary tent!

Signal Fires

There may be little or no occasion to use the smoke signal fire, but it may be of historical interest to know how it was done and, perhaps, as civilization's progress turns back upon itself and we return to natural ways, it may once again be a tool for communication. Signal fires were set in the daylight and at high elevations. Their range was between 20 and 50 miles (32–80km). They were constructed by placing four green or wet stakes 3 feet (.9m) high and 3 feet apart in a square formation. Four lighter green stakes were lashed between them near the top. A small, hot fire was erected in the center of the square, and a pile of slow fuel—grass, leaves and green sticks—laid over the top. The frame was covered with a smoke cloth made of burlap or canvas 8 × 8 feet (2.4 × 2.4m) in size with a hole cut in the center and anchored on the ground with stones. Laid over this structure was a signal cloth large enough to cover the smoke hole and drape over the sides slightly.

To signal, the smoke hole was covered with the wet cloth for approximately 30 seconds, then quickly swung upward. A second later the sender hit the side of the covered cloth with a stout branch beater. The message was determined by the number of signals, their strength and form—balls, columns, and spirals—and the color of the smoke which was changed by adding different herbs to the fire.

For fun and simple signaling you might work out a family or group code for camping and try decifering one another's smoke signals. A simpler signaling device may be rigged with just a green branch fire, a wet canvas smoke cloth, and two persons each holding two corners of the cloth. This type of communication is strenuous, so keep it short and sweet.

A friendly fire is the camper's companion. It is a tool to be used as carefully as an ax or knife and one to be completely eliminated before moving on. Douse your campfire with water, lightly scatter the ashes, and douse again. Don't forget to erase all, or as many as possible, of your fire's traces. Consider the consequences.

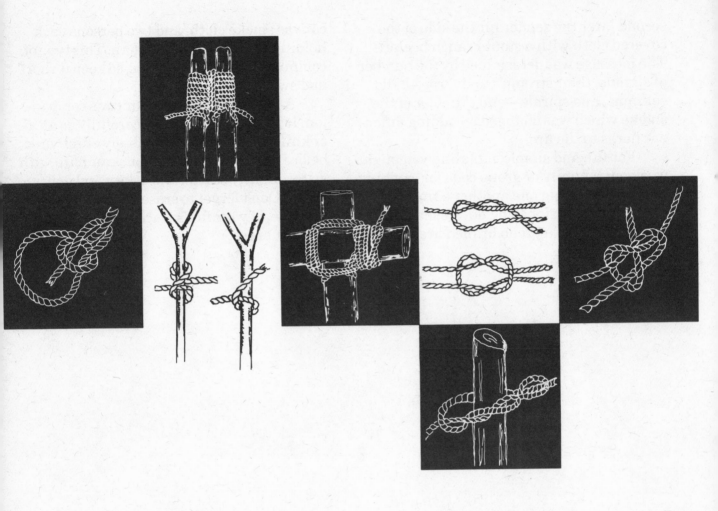

4

Knots and Lashings

Among the thousands of knots and lashings which have been developed, you should need only a half dozen or so to complete the projects described in this book.

Selection of a secure rope is the first consideration. (See Chapter 1.) If you are using hemp you may determine its strength in American measuring units by squaring the diameter and multiplying that number by 7200. The safety factor is a quarter of the breaking strength. For example: ¼-inch rope × ¼ inch × 7200 breaks at 450 pounds. Divided by four, the safety limit is 112 pounds. Braided nylon of the same diameter supports three times that of hemp, or 336 pounds.

If the rope is going to break, it will generally come apart at the knot.

Knots

The best woodcraft knots can replace nails, are easy to tie, hold securely or slip as

needed, and are easy to untie. Hemp, which is good for pole lashings, securing bundles and tent guys, needs only a simple knot to hold it. Nylon, which is suitable for lashing backpack loads among other projects, is slippery and requires more complicated knots. (Actually the best knot for nylon is a combination of easy and intricate knots.) The purpose of knots is to attach one piece of rope to another without splicing or to attach a piece of rope to a stationary object. The reference to standing end means the stationary end of the rope around which the knot is fashioned. The working end is the movable part of the rope which meanders in and out of loops to make the various knots. Refer to the accompanying illustrations for clarification.

Proper preparation of the rope will add to its longevity and its efficiency. To stop fraying, make the rope easier to handle, and facilitate grommet threading, you will want to whip the rope ends. You may use any strong string, waxed or plain. Make a short loop at one end of the string, laying it along the top of the rope end. Holding one end in your left hand, wind the free string end several times around the loop and rope with your right. Pull the left free end straight. The loop will be pulled under the coils and the other free end secured. Trim the ends.

A stopper knot will also prevent your rope from fraying. Untwist the rope strands at one end a few inches in. Lay them flat and parallel to the direction of the rope. Tie a single overhand knot and pull it tight against the open end. Roll the knot underfoot to make it smooth and tight.

Square knot

Square Knot:

The basic square knot is used to connect two lines of equal diameter and of the same material together. It is dependable as a tie for packs and bundles and is easy to execute.

1. Take the ends of two ropes in either hand and cross them one over the other.
2. Pass the first under the second (right under left) and point both ends up.
3. Now, reversing the direction, cross the new right over the left, passing it under and around in a "double granny."

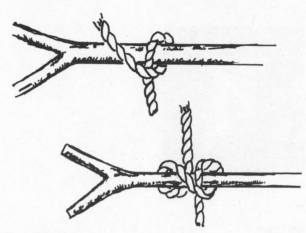

Clove hitch

Clove Hitch:

This is a line knot to hold an elevated food cache, secure a rope to or around a branch or secure one line to another. Able to be used horizontally or vertically, the clove hitch is a good, fast knot important to lashing operations.

1. Loop the rope around the stationary rope or branch working from the front over the top, under and up, crossing over the standing end and to the left.
2. Repeat the loop in the front but in mirror image and ending with the working end pointing upward.
3. Tighten the knot by squeezing the loops together while pulling on the ends.

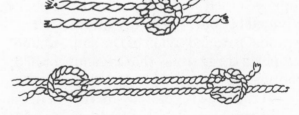

Fisherman's Knot

Fisherman's Knot:

This knot is especially good for tying vines together and joins two pieces of rope or cording with more authority than a square knot.

1. Run two lines parallel to one another and make a loop of one around the other.
2. Repeat making a loop in the second line around the first.
3. Tighten the loops separately; pull them together and tighten each again.

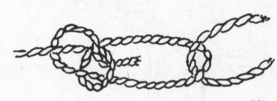

Slip Knot

Bowline

Bowline: The bowline works well as a non-slip loop at the end of a line. It may be used to attach guylines to tent loops, to tie one loop to another or to secure one end of a clothes line to a tree.

1. Hold the long end of the rope in the left hand forming a loop on the right side of the rope, short line on top.
2. Loop short (top) line around or through the object to be secured.
3. Run the short end up through the loop, around the standing end and back down through the loop.

   "The rabbit comes up out of his hole, around the tree and back down in his hole" is one way to help children and kids-at-heart knotters remember the sequence of turns.

Slip Knot: For fastening a line to a pole, and for other situations where there is a constant pull to hold the knot taught, the slip knot is a good choice.

1. Double a length of rope back upon itself, the working end over the standing end.
2. Push the working end up through the loop, over the outer loop, and under and up through the loop.

Sheet Bend

Sheet Bend: This knot is especially good for wet or frozen rope and for connecting rope of different sizes. It is simple to do, will not slip, and unties in a jiffy.

1. Make a loop in one rope.
2. Bring the end of the other rope up through the loop and around the standing end.
3. Pass the end of the second rope under itself where it comes up through the loop.

Timber Hitch

Double Half Hitch

Timber Hitch: The timber hitch is good for securing vines and other green materials. A major lashing knot, it is used to fasten a rope to a pole. It needs tightening to be secure.

1. Pass the rope around the pole.
2. Make a half hitch around the standing end.

3. Take three or more turns under and around the loop.
4. Draw tight keeping a constant pressure on the new knot.
5. Pull the loop to loosen and remove.

Half Hitch:

1. Pass the cord or rope around the object to be tied.
2. Bring the end back and around the standing end.
3. Push the end down through the loop.
4. Repeat for a double half hitch.

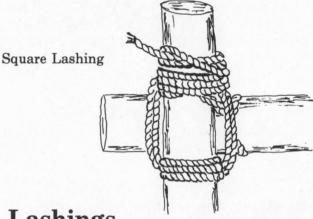

Square Lashing

Lashings

There are two major lashings used for making stools, tables, washstands, chairs, rafts, bedsteads, etc. Both work best using twine up to ½ inch (12.5mm) thick, the project itself determining the strength of cord needed.

Square Lashing: The square lashing is the easiest and is good for constructing lean-tos or other projects which require holding two bracing poles together at irregular angles or "cross purposes."

1. Cross the poles.
2. Hook the rope to one pole with a clove or timber hitch.

3. Take three turns around all the joint arms both vertically and horizontally.
4. End with two or three frapping turns (winding rope between the poles) to tighten the lashing and secure the work with two half hitches or a clove hitch around one pole.

Shear Lashing: The shear lash is designed to join two to three poles end to end or side by side.

1. Secure one pole with a clove or timber hitch.
2. Wrap the rope around the poles five to eight times.
3. Frap turn between the poles two to three times to bind the lash.
4. Finish with a clove hitch on the opposite pole.

Mastered, these simple knots and lashings will keep the pack on your back and the tarp overhead. As their loops and turns become second nature, you will become free of the mechanics of outdoor life and be able to simply be, as other creatures are, in and of the woods and wilderness.

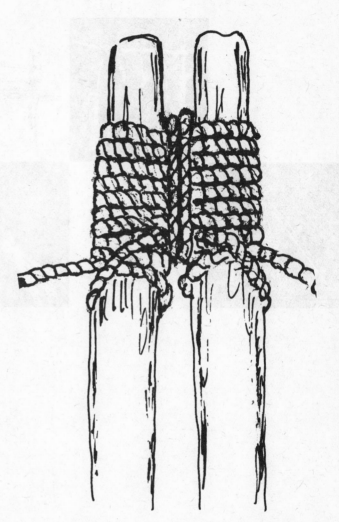

Shear Lashing

5

The Comfortable Campsite

It is irresponsible to sleep where you drop from exhaustion on a camping expedition; you should not get that tired. Stopping early in the day and planning a shelter and campsite are vital to enjoying outdoor living. In the wilds, look for a suitable water supply, level ground, the availability of wood for fire and shelter, and note the prevalence of insects. All are factors in your future comfort even if that future is only overnight.

The best real estate is land that drains away from any nearby lake or stream. In the desert, find a cacti-free place where there is fuel and material to form a windbreak. A sheltered knoll in a patch of sagebrush is ideal. You may use your tarp as ground cover and pocket yourself in a sleeping bag to keep off the dew. A small, open space on level ground is the site to seek in the high mountains. And you do not need to know how to float to get a night's rest in the swamp. Even there, it usually is possible to find respectably dry land. Locate the highest

possible level; a ridge between waters will do.

A comfortable camp can be set up easily along a river and by the sea. High gravel bars are good sites. And you can cozy up to a pile of driftwood which has been brought down and deposited by spring floods. It offers a windbreak as well as fuel. Just attend to the high waterline and sleep above it.

Tarp Tenting

Going from basic to better tarp shelters, we begin with a simple shelter utilizing a fallen log. Overlay the fallen log with the tarp, pinning down the sides tight and staking the grommets with pegs. With only a small clearance between tarp and ground, this is a sleeping shelter only. A roomier frame may be made by securing one end of a sapling to a blown down tree with the other end propped up by two short poles. This type provides a living space approximately 3 feet (.9m) high and 5 feet (1.5m) wide.

A basic tarp and log "tent"

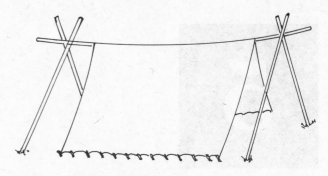

Double A-frame tarp tent

The following styles are one-person arrangements which suit themselves to changing weather and terrain. They generally utilize a 9 × 12-foot (2.7 × 3.6m) tarp and can be erected in 4–5 minutes:

1. A simple roof shelter may be made by lashing the tarp to four available trees or by cutting stakes and setting them at appropriate corners.

2. Erect a wood pole frame consisting of two long and two shorter poles set in a square. Lay and lash cross poles between the forward (long) two poles and between the back (shorter) two. Stretch the tarp from the forward pole to the back pole and secure it at the ground. You may leave the sides open or lash several horizontal sticks on each side and weave boughs or leafy branches among them.

3. Measure the distance between two trees and cut a pole to match. Lash the pole to short pegs set at a distance behind the two trees. Tie a tarp corner at the base of each tree and pull the cloth back and under the pegged pole. Stretch the tarp over the pole and forward, tying the remaining ends to the trees high enough to provide sheltered seating. You now have a roof and ground cover in one.

4. A familiar tent-like shelter can be made by constructing two A-frames of straight sticks. Connect them with a top pole and lash several horizontal branches down the side. To cover, lay the tarp over the top of the structure and secure the sides on the ground with logs or stakes through the eyelets. A variation of this design may be constructed as illustrated.

5. Even a tepee can be constructed in record time by lashing four to six light logs pyramid-style at the top. Starting at one side, lash the tarp to one upright log and pull the tarp around. Lash that end of the tarp to its adjacent log. You may leave the door free or prop leafy branches in the opening to keep the weather out.

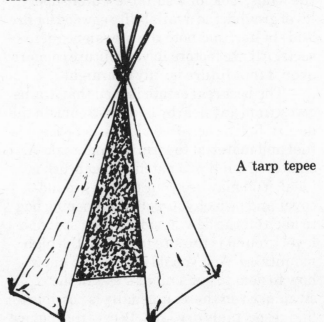

A tarp tepee

6. For cold, windy nights a tarp tunnel is a good bet. Bend a sapling into an arch and stake it down keeping the opening downwind. Lash the tarp to the sapling, pull it straight back and stake it. Secure the side grommets with pegs and brace the front with a cord running from the center of the sapling arch to a peg in the ground several feet in front of the shelter. (This same shelter may be made using a lashed three-stick doorframe rather than a sapling archway.) Take care not to break or otherwise kill any saplings you use.

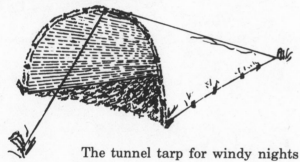

The tunnel tarp for windy nights

7. Another simple tarp tent sets you up to sleep with your head high . . . at the foot of a tree. Tie a straight pole to a tree trunk 6 feet (1.8m) from the ground. Peg the bottom and wrap the tarp around the pole with the tree at the mouth of the tent. Tie one end of the tarp near the tree at the top of the sapling and secure the bottom at the end of the

sapling. Spread the loose ends and tie them down. Because of the danger of lightning, this style is not recommended in a thunderstorm.

8. The tarp tent above may also be made using two front prop poles instead of a tree. This gives more room at the front including space for a warming fire. An added variation to this style turns the shelter into a gypsy tent. To the two straight forward branches is added a third, forked branch of equal length. Set into a tripod, a 10–14-foot (3.0–4.2m) cord is stretched from the tripod to windward. The tarp is dropped over the taut cord and staked down at the sides. Under the tripod lies the fire and over the fire hangs a pot: a self-contained outdoor apartment—fire, food, and shelter within reach.

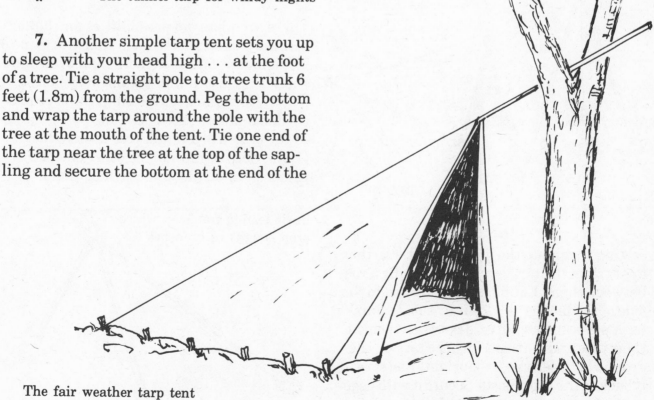

The fair weather tarp tent

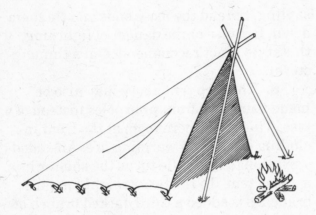

A front-prop tarp tent

9. Using a bit more wood and work, you may make a tarp Taj Mahal. Cut four equally long poles and lash them in twos,

up the back stay, and over the rod set between the main braces. You will now have a ground cover, a backdrop, and a partially peaked room. You may finish this fancy place by staking out the overhang with cords and pegs to the front as shown.

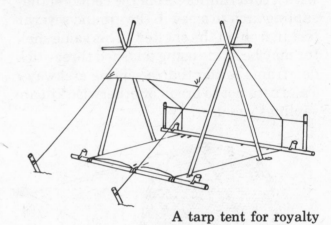

A tarp tent for royalty

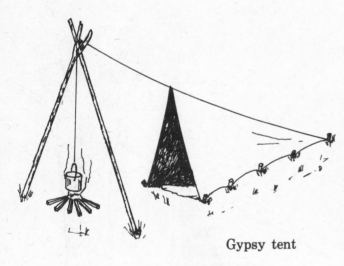

Gypsy tent

setting them into the ground a little farther apart than the tarp is wide and laying a rod between them. Equidistant apart and to the side of the facing "A's," put in 1-foot (.3m) high posts and string cord between them at their tops and bottoms. Lay the tarp on the ground between the "A" uprights and spread it back to the short posts. Secure it with pegs at the front and run it under the bottom cord,

Lean-Tos

There are plenty of possibilities for shelter sans tarp using just what is handy. A lean-to is not meant for much more than overnight shelter . . . a two-night stand at the most.

1. The quickest is a simple and practical den made of a 20-foot (6.0m) pole leaning in the crotch of a larger tree about 5 feet (1.5m) above ground. The other end of the pole is pointed and pierces the ground.

Basic lean-to frame on which prop boughs or branches

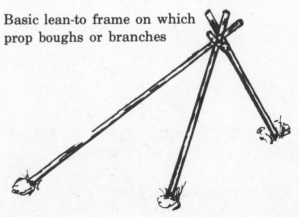

Tree pole wigwam

Against this single rib lean bush fir or hemlock branches to enclosed a comfortable space. (Two crossed poles may replace the tree as shown in the illustration.)

2. A variation of this produces a wigwam effect. Instead of just one pole leaning in the crotch of the tree, several more are set in a semi-circle and the available boughs are woven in between the branches rather than laid on. This takes a bit longer but provides a little more room inside.

3. The tree serves as a brace for still another lean-to style. Two poles are cut a bit more than 4 feet (1.2m) long, lashed together in a "A" outline, and set into the ground several feet from the tree. A cross piece is lashed in the fork of the poles and to the tree at the same height. Identically long

branches are lashed side by side to the cross piece and driven into the ground 6 feet (1.8m) behind the uprights to form the back ribs of the lean-to. Side braces may be cut and secured vertically to hold thatching for added enclosure. Poles parallel to the upper cross pieces may be added and lashed a foot (.3m) apart down the ribs for still more thatching area. (This same lean-to may be put up using two trees or two forked sticks rather than a tree and two braced sticks.)

A lean-to frame with bough thatch samples

Lean-to with thatched side

Thatching

The Irish have used thatched coverings for years; there's no more natural way to keep dry. In the wilderness, the best thatching material includes balsam, spruce, fir, pine, broad leaves, long and rolled grasses, long-stalked fern and palm fronds, to name a few. Dry or partly dry material is preferred to green because as green material dries it shrinks and reduces the area of coverage. If green material is the only kind available, cut it a bit ahead of time, if possible, to allow it to dry, and secure it tightly. Coverage

rather than thickness is what counts, and the pattern of thatching from bottom to top, with each successive layer covering the one below it, provides the best waterproofing.

To secure the thatching material you may set it to the cross battens using an 18-inch (45cm) "needle" made from wood. Cut a straight grained and dead stick 1 inch (2.5cm) thick to the designated length,

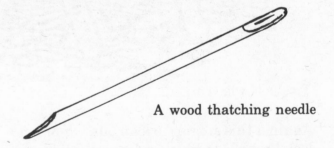

A wood thatching needle

sharpen one end, and rub it smooth. Whittle the other end to a ¼ inch (6.25mm) thickness for about 3 inches (7.5cm). Bore an "eye" ¼ inch (6.25cm) wide and ½ inch (12.5mm) long in that end. Thread the needle with a length of cording and attach the end of the thatching batten with a timber hitch knot.

Piercing the thatching material at a slant, secure it to the batten one row at a time.

A stick overlay may be used instead of the sewing method. Secure a thin stick to the batten at one end. Lay thatching material along the batten to the length of the stick and tie the stick down at its end, thus holding the thatching material in place.

Grass thatch sheaves on a lean-to wall

Using reeds or coarse grasses gathered in sheaves about 1 inch (2.5cm) thick, you may tuft-thatch a wilderness roof and side wall. Bend one end of the sheave over the batten and secure it by twisting several strands around the main and overlapped ends to hold. There's no need to wad the sheaves too tightly. Placement an inch (2.5cm) apart is sufficient to keep you dry in any weather. If the grasses you are working with tend to cut, wear gloves to protect your hands.

In broadleaf country you can thatch using single leaves overlaid and sewn on the batten one at a time with a sliver of bark. Oceanside you may thatch a lean-to roof using palm fronds the center ribs of which have been split (but not separated) and laid straddling the batten so that the leaves are overlapping one another.

Although an excellent cover, thatching does introduce a hazard. Beware of making your fire too close to a thatched structure which has dried in the sun for several days. The danger of fire is considerable.

Bush Shelter

During the summer a bush hut can be made by bending the leafy branches of a pliable, tall shrub in an arch to the ground. Secure it with pegs and thongs. Be careful not to crack the branches as you bend them, and remember to untie the structure to allow it to return to its original shape once you have finished with it. Other branches may be woven among the arched ones to add windproofing as needed.

To add the finishing touch to all of the above improvisations, pile dirt around the outside edges of the structures. In winter, snow may be substituted to a height of 3–5 inches (7.5–12.5cm) to insulate the structure.

Sun Screen

For a family used to living in a many-roomed house, being confined to a squat and single-room lean-to may prove hazardous to mental health. Also, you may need only sun shelter during the day and may not want to huddle in a hot tarp lean-to. The shade tepee is ideal in both cases. Prop 12 to 16 16-foot (4.8m) fallen saplings together in a cone shape. Cover them with a 10 to 12 foot (3.0–3.6m) canvas tied to the poles with cording or birch bark strips. Or, lay leafy boughs against the poles if the tarp is too much. The structure, because there are few or no lashings, is easily moved as the sun changes and is a good site for crafts, games, and afternoon naps.

Palm Frond Tepee

If you should be so "lucky" as to be stranded on a desert island, here is how to get in out of the glare. Hollow out a cool nest in the sand about 4 feet (1.2m) in diameter and a foot (.3m) deep. Collect eight or more long palm fronds, bunch them up and tie the small ends together with cording. Stand this dense wigwam up in the middle of your hole, butt ends down, and carefully spread the branches out and over the hole. Push the end of each frond into the sand 2–3 inches (5.0–7.5cm) to hold the hut stable. Crawl in, lay back, and wait to be saved.

Beds

If you make one one stick of furniture for your overnight stay, it should be a bed. You can sit on a log and eat off your knee, but you should get a good night's rest. Basic bedding may be built of balsam fir, or spruce boughs. Make sure the butt ends point toward the earth and are covered with additional layers to a foot (.3m) or more deep. Your rest should be comfortable for at least a couple of nights. Bough cutting is forbidden by law in many places and by conservation in others. If you are on land where such cutting is permitted, it's still a good idea to collect only the lower boughs of evergreens. To carry them back to your campsite, lay the crotches over the handle of your ax. Other materials which can soften your sleep are dry moss, sweet scented pine needles, leaves, fern, and marsh hay.

Frontier Stick Bed

To raise those boughs up off the ground, you may construct a stick bed like those once used by the pioneers. Three feet (.925m) apart, stake down two parallel logs, 6–7 inches (15.0–17.5cm) thick and 7 feet (2.1m) long. Cross them with 20–30 springy sticks about 3½ feet (1.05m) long and 4 inches (10.0cm) apart. Then notch four logs, two long and two short, 3–4 inches (7.5–10.0cm) thick to form an upper mattress frame. Make a pillow at the head end using stacked 6-inch (15.0cm) cross sticks. Fill in over the stick "springs" with dry leaves, fern, spruce or balsam boughs, sucker growth, weeds, bush material or other available vegetation which promises to be comfortable.

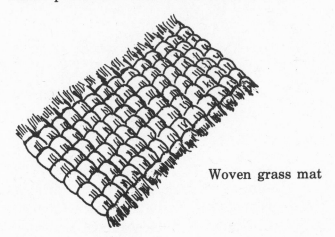

Woven grass mat

Grass Mat

For the sleeper whose limit of roughing it is reached far before bedtime, the grass mattress is a good investment of time and effort. The mat begins with a weaving frame made by setting stakes at the head and at the foot of the intended bed size. Two cords are run from each stake to its opposite, and additional cords are strung between the first two about an inch apart. Grasses are gathered in clumps 30 inches (75.0cm) long and 3 inches

(7.5cm) in diameter and are inserted alternately over and under the cords across the width and down the length of the bed. When the stuffing is finished, remove the mat from the stakes, tie the cords off at the ends, and slide it under a sleepy person.

With the cord draped to the left, Mint prepares to take a stitch in the hammock weave.

Mint Ulmanis weaves a web of nylon cording soon to be a hammock for open air sleeping.

Holding the new thread firm with his left thumb, he is ready to go on.

Hammocks

With the new consciousness of the environment steering wanderers to low-impact camping, the hammock comes into its own. Any type of strong cording may be used to make the hammock, but Mint Ulmanis of Lake Zurich, Illinois, prefers nylon to reproduce the fishing net weave his grandfather taught him when he was a small boy

The hanging stick 'n' bark bed

in Latvia. In addition to cord you will need a hardwood shuttle (birch, maple, or oak are examples) whittled as shown in the photographs and a lay-over wood piece 8 inches (20.0cm) long and 1½ inches (6.25cm) wide. (A longer lay-over will give you more room for a wider hammock.)

The cord is either wrapped around a convenient tree or attached to a hook on the tree, and then wrapped in a figure eight on either side of the smoothed shuttle.

To begin, hold the layover wood piece in the left hand with the cord laying overtop and the shuttle in the right hand. Draw the cord under the layover wood and bring it up looping a coil over your left hand and pulling the shuttle through the prepared loop. Re-

peat as many times as you like; then slip the first row off the layover piece and, starting a new row, catch the successive loops of the first row last to first. When you have made the length of hammock you wish—7 feet (2.1m) is a good sleeping length—merely tie off the end and loop the first and last lines through smoothed, short, stout branches and hang with rope from the nearest trees. Fishing nets may be made the same way using finer cord. Patience makes the product; that and 6 hours of work, so do not wait until the sun sinks to start this sleeping accommodation. Of course, commercially produced hammocks are relatively inexpensive and are generally small enough to tuck into the corner of a backpack.

Stick 'n' Bark Hammock

Using a camp loom (described below), weave a 6½-foot (1.95m) long and 3-foot (.914m) wide hammock of 1-inch (2.5cm) thick sticks and vines, twisted bark, or grass rope. Finish the ends with 2-inch (5.0cm) thick spreaders connected to short pieces of rope at either end and finally connected to the main ropes which are tied to appropriately spaced trees. For added comfort, cover the sticks with a grass mat.

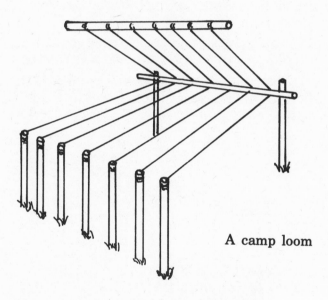

A camp loom

Camp Loom: To construct a camp loom, drive two sticks into the ground about 6 inches (15.0cm) wider than the hammock or grass mat is to be wide. Lash a strong, trimmed and smoothed cross piece between the forks which are set to the back. Now, cut straight stakes 2–3 feet (.6–.925m) long and set them into the ground 8–9 feet (2.4–2.7m) in front of the cross bar and 2–3 inches (5.0–7.5cm) apart. Cut another cross bar about 3–4 inches (7.5–10.0cm) longer than the row of front stakes is wide and lay it on the ground in front of them. To set the loom's warp, attach cording to each front stake and

run it back to the cross bar and tie it on. Another set of warp cords half again as long as the first are fastened to the back bar and to the movable front cross bar lying on the ground.

Two people may work this loom easily. While one lifts the movable warp above the stationary one, the second person places even sticks or bunches of hay, cattails, or rushes between the cord at the end nearest the back bar. When one row is complete, the first weaver drops the movable warp cords below the stationary cords and the sticks or grasses are laid in a second row. The weaving continues in this fashion, alternating the insertion of the grasses above and below the doubled cords. When the desired length is achieved, the warp ends are cut and tied together and the mat is taken from the frame, side ends trimmed, and then used for anything from a mattress, rug, or door curtain to a window shade.

Make a mosquito net bar for undisturbed nights.

Mosquito Bar

For sleeping-bag-only campers, who, despite their hardiness, are kept awake by the drone of mosquitoes, the following apparatus is suggested. Bring from home several yards of dark mosquito netting or dyed cheese cloth sewn into rectangles or pup-tent triangles. (Dark material can be seen through better and does not attract pesky insects.) Construct a frame of two forked sticks set in the ground on either side of the head of your bag with a cross piece connecting them. Simply slip into your bag and drape the netting over the two forked sticks. You may raise the netting a bit above your head and shoulders by adding another forked stick set on either side of the bag a bit lower down.

The Kitchen

As you make your home away from home, your next step is to the kitchen. Unless you have constructed one of the tarp or lean-tos incorporating a campfire and kitchen at your doorstep, you must now set up your camp cooking area. Besides the considerations to be made for safety as mentioned in Chapter 3, set up your kitchen with a wet finger to the prevailing wind and an eye on your sleeping quarters. Don't build a fire where smoke will blow into the area.

Your kitchen can be as simple as a pot on a tripod or as fancy as a French chef's. The tepee fire with the low hanging pot as described in Chapter 3 may be embellished if you select branches with natural hooks. From these you may hang pot holders, drying clothes, and cooking pans. A larger kitchen may be made using four green poles with natural branch hooks. Rest or lash cross sticks to frame a square near the top and again lower down toward the fire. Dry dish towels above and pots from the side hooks.

A well-equipped wilderness kitchen provides areas for drying and storing utensils, as well as eating.

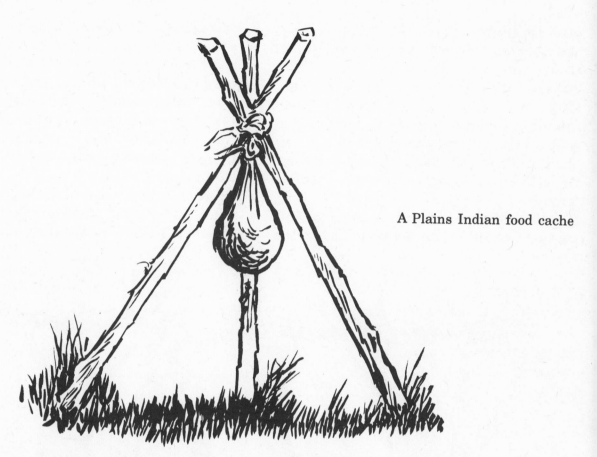

A Plains Indian food cache

For a touch of wilderness class, you may construct a sideboard for your dining space. Find two forked sticks 3 feet (.925m) long and two between 3 and 4 feet (.925–1.2m) in length. Set the forked sticks into the ground near your eating and cooking area and post the two taller sticks about 2 feet (.6m) behind them. Join all four with cross poles forming a rectangle. Lash a longer cross pole to the top of the back poles and fill in the rectangular surface area with close-set sticks the length of the structure, notching or lashing to hold. Here you may dry your camp crockery and store your pots and pans for easy accessibility. If the filler branches on the surface of the sideboard are close enough together you can even hang the cutlery. From a back-branch extension dry a dish towel, a wet bathing suit, or hangered clothes. Improvise.

Caches

And what is a kitchen without cupboard space? A challenge. To store foodstuffs close at hand but up and out of the way of roving bears and other bandits, there are a variety of caches to choose from. The simplest was used by the Plains Indians and was merely a tall tripod with food hanging in a bundle from the upper fork. When trees are available you can protect your larder by tying a bundle at the top of a pole. Hoist the other end up into the crotch of a tree branch and push it through so the butt end rests on the ground on the other side. To retrieve the food just reverse the process. Staples may also be stored among the branches of a young tree. Bend a sapling over gently, attach the food bundle and release the tree. This cache is safe from all but squirrels and ants.

Ingenuity or experience offers still another food saver. Find a pole long enough to rest in the crotches of adjacent trees. Hoist it into place with the help of a forked pole. Tie your food into a waterproof pouch and secure the end with a rope. Throw the free end of the rope over the overhead pole and pull on it until the food bag is a few inches from the pole. Lash the rope end to one of the trees.

A wilderness cooler is possible to construct. Cut four poles and set them into the ground at a comfortable height and in a square. Connect the poles with four shorter poles to form the bottom of a box. Fill in the box sides, bottom and top with sticks of the same size. Thatch the roof with boughs and set a water-filled coffee can on top. Immerse the ends of clean rags in the water and let them hang over the sides and onto the thatching. Cover the front of the cooler with a piece of oilcloth, canvas, or leafy branches. Set up in the shade, this camp "refrigerator" should register a temperature 20–40

Hanging food caches

Camp "refrigerator" uses evaporating water to provide coolness

degrees lower than the outside shade. (This same structure may also be suspended from an overhead pole to keep it safe from critters.)

Skim the soap off the surface and scrub your duds with that. A wilderness washboard can even be made out of available materials. Take a slab of hardwood and peel off the bark. Cut grooves on the curved surface of the board by notching the length of it and rounding off the sharp edges.

And finally, for pins to hang those clean clothes on a tree-to-tree clothes cord, take short, green sticks, split one end and remove the bark (to avoid stains) from that end. Hang 'em up, dry 'em out, put 'em on. And you are ready for a trip to town or a second wind in the woods.

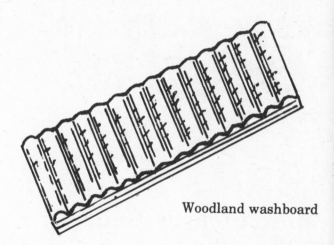

Woodland washboard

Soap and Laundry

Assuming that roughing it means living in as few changes of clothes as outdoor etiquette will indulge, you probably will not need to do laundry in the backwoods. But, should you want to and be without means, there is an answer as close as the campfire. A prairie "soap" is made by pouring boiling water through the wood ashes several times. Your clothes will come clean in the water alone. To make "real" soap along the way, boil wood ash water with a small amount of bacon grease until the water is almost gone.

Water

If nearby water is of questionable drinking quality you can filter it to safeguard your health. Simply set four stakes into the ground and lash four more near the top to form a square on legs. Attach a light, non-waterproof cloth to the four cords and fill the bottom of it with sand or cold charcoals. Pour your suspicious water through this apparatus to remove mud, stones, and other solid matter. The water should then be boiled for 10 minutes to guard against bacterial impurities.

Camp purification system

More Utensils, Gadgets, and Gear

Admittedly, a knife is a handy thing, but you cannot cook much with or on it, and it does not hold a meal unless you are strictly a honey and peas person. So your camp kitchen and related activities will require a few more homemade items to get the eats out and to let you live the leisure life in the woods.

Pot Hooks: These are basic essentials for suspending pots and pans over hot fires. You should have a variety of them in lengths from 6 to 10 inches (15–25cm) and ½ inch (12.5mm) in diameter. Each piece of green wood should have a natural hook at one end.

You provide the pot slot by cutting a notch in the opposite direction of the hook, on the other side and at the other end. A loop and hook is another handy variation. Take a sapling branch with a fork and shorten one tine. Gently bend the long shoot around and secure it to its base. You now have a loop with a hook on it which may be used on a mounted pole above a fire.

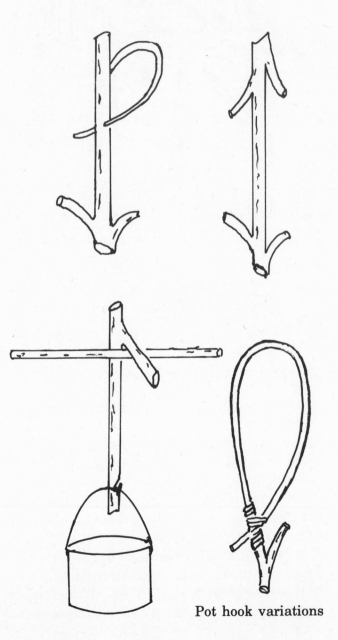

Pot hook variations

The "tennis racket" grill

Spit: For hare kabobs or camp bread, you may construct a simple spit using two forked branches set on either side of a fire. Across them lay a straight branch with an offshoot at one end offering a handle. Turn the bread constantly for even cooking.

Toasters: Toast for breakfast is practically a luxury when camping out, but it is easy if you have the right props. Find two sticks with forks. Trim them to little more than bread slice size and whittle a point at the bottom of each stick. Set them in the ground near the fire and place a slice of bread in the crook of the sticks. Turn the bread to toast both sides. A hand held three-tined fork with the bread wedged in will also do the trick.

Bowls: The burls of birch, cherry, apple, oak, or maple can provide you with a bowl for your cereal or supper soup. Noggins (bowls with handles) are made of tree growths which appear as knobs or large warts on the bark. To fashion your own noggin, select a burl slightly larger than the

Grills: For specialized cooking you may make the "tennis rackets" of the forest, woven fork grills. Again, find a sapling with a fork. Heat the stick to make it pliable and bend the longest and outside tine around the other securing it in the crotch with a cord (if necessary). Using ¼-inch (13.75mm) diameter green sticks, weave the racket to form a grillwork. A "Y" shaped fork may also be used without bending as a frank fork. A three-tined fork offers another type. You may leave the tines as they are or weave in green sticks for a more solid grill surface.

Triple tine fork

A tree burl used for noggins and spoons

Triple tine fork with green sticks
weaved in creates a more solid surface

object you wish to make. Test it for rot by scraping the bark off and pressing it to determine whether there are any soft spots. Remove the burl from the tree with your saw as close to the trunk as possible. To provide yourself with a handle, extend the cut as illustrated. Cover the tree's wound with paint or tar to heal.

Burls are more easily worked when they are green. You simply carve out the bowl to the depth you wish, soak it in linseed oil or bacon fat and hang it up to dry. If the burl is from a dry, hardwood tree, it will take a bit more muscle. Bore holes in the mass and chisel out as much wood as possible. A crooked knife works well. If the working of the noggin takes more than one sitting, submerge the burl in linseed oil or water to prevent it from cracking between whittlings. Round off and sand the edges smooth and bore a hole in the handle to hang it from your belt by a thong. When the carving is done, remove the bark, soak it overnight in oil, and hang it to dry thoroughly. The noggin may then be polished with leather or a mixture of turpentine and beeswax.

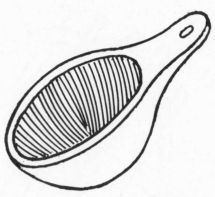

A finished burl noggin

Noggins may even be personalized with your own abstract design using grease and woodsmoke. Cover the outside of a design area of the bowl with grease and hold it over a slow burning, greenwood fire. When the bowl is dark, remove it from the fire and rub it vigorously with a clean cloth.

A larger bowl for soup, salad, or stew also can be made of seasoned hard- or softwood 9–10 inches (22 to 25cm) square and 2 inches (5cm) thick. (The Chippewa preferred ash, maple, or birch using the trunk section just above the ground.)

A large bowl for soup, salad or stew

Draw an outline for the bowl and, using a gouge or knife, cut out a depression in the piece, working in a circular pattern. Sand the edges and corners smooth and rub the new bowl with vegetable oil to coat it. You may make your own oil using sunflower seeds, hickory nuts, walnuts, or beechnuts. Boil the nuts in water, skimming and saving the oil from the surface.

The Indians call it a "colamin." They make a dish out of a flat rectangular piece of green tree bark. Softening it with their hands, they fold it (as shown) and fasten the ends at the top with a sharp peg or tree thorn. The Iroquois made a functional bowl of elm bark and spruce roots. They soaked the material in hot water to make it pliable and fan-folded both ends, binding them with roots. The middle was flared open to form a bowl.

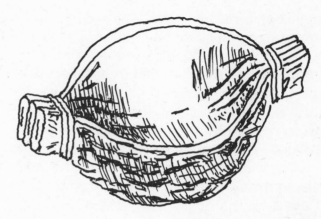

An Iroquois bark bowl

A birch bowl is made by cutting out a circular or oval pattern from a piece of flat bark. Into each quarter, cut an even slot. The evenness is important as it determines the slope of the bowl's sides. Bend the four sides up and stitch or secure them with a thorn peg.

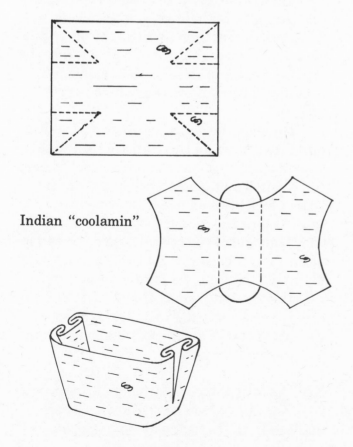

Indian "coolamin"

Oval birch bowl

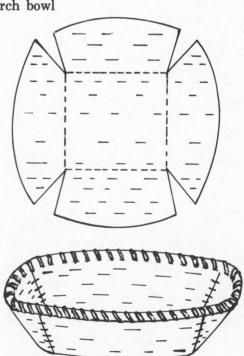

Bowls may be individualized by decorating them with a prepared pattern. Cut out a flower, an eagle on the wing, or your own personal symbol from a piece of discarded bark. Trace the design on the side of your bowl and carefully scrape the inner design area out, removing one or two layers of bark. Dampening helps the scraping. You will now have a light design against a dark background and your "name" on your "plate."

Simple designs for personalizing your bark bowl

The Chippewas, known as the "birch bark Indians," knew much more of the birch craft. They gathered the bark in the early summer when the sap was up in the tree and the bark came away clean. With a knife, the gatherer made a slightly curved longitudinal cut in the tree bark. He then worked it away from the tree using the knife and the flat of his hand. Utensils as described above and below were laced with the tough and flexible roots of the black spruce. These roots, found in the moist soil near the ground's surface and where stream erosion had exposed them, were gathered in the spring. They were soaked for several days, scraped clean of their bark, and split lengthwise. When black spruce roots were unavailable, the roots of white cedar or tamarack were substituted.

To further prepare the bowls for cooking and eating, they were sealed with pitch. Spruce or pine gum was collected from a split in the tree. The sticky, flammable material was then carefully heated until it became a liquid and was daubed into the seams of the birch containers.

Making an Eena: To make an eena, or root bark remover, split a stick at one end and tie the shaft below the split to keep it from tearing further. Whittle the other end of the stick into a point and shove it into the ground. Insert in the eena just above the binding the end of the root which is to be stripped.

Holding the eena jaws with your left hand, pull the root through the split with your right. (This operation also may be accomplished using a notched board and a short block of wood to exert pressure.)

To split the lacing roots, make a cut in the large end of the root and hold the end in your teeth. Below the cut hold the root with your right thumb and forefinger and separate the root with a long thumb nail. The left hand draws away the root strand being worked. Take your time to make maximum length root thongs.

Kettles and Pans: Although it may seem hard to believe, you can cook with a pan made of bark. In fact, you can make a cook-

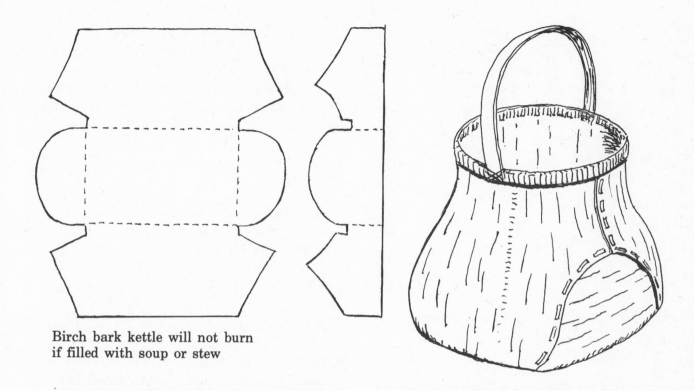

Birch bark kettle will not burn
if filled with soup or stew

ing pan just as the Chippewa and Menomini used. Cut a sheet of bark 7–10 inches (17–25cm) wide, 20 inches (50cm) long, and 8 inches (20.0cm) deep. Prepare as described above folding the corners in a "v" angle and taking several stitches with a root cord. Fill it with soup or stew and drop in red hot stones, continuing to do so until the meal is hot.

A kettle may be made in any size you wish, using the design shown here. Soften the birch bark with water and punch holes as indicated with your knife blade. Fold the forming kettle up and stitch it using root cord, leather thongs, or nylon cord; then, waterproof the seams. You can strengthen the top of the kettle with a bent willow branch attached with an overhand stitch with more root cord. To make the kettle handy to use, improvise a handle from a second willow branch and lash it soundly to both sides. You can cook with a birch bark kettle even over an open flame, just as long

as the fire does not reach above the liquid line.

Spoons: Soup's on and served, but what is needed next is a spoon to eat it with. Several woodcraft spoons are possible:

Locate a basswood, cedar, or maple stump and cut a 7½ × 2½ inch (19 × 7cm) piece of wood from the ground level trunk. This section provides the best grain, and its turning toward the roots makes the angle natural for a spoon. Remove the bark and trace the spoon shape as shown. Saw out the rough form, leaving a triangle at the base to lend support while you are whittling out the bowl. Now, whittle the finer lines with your knife and rub the whole piece with linseed oil. After allowing the spoon to dry for several days, sand it, rub in more oil, and polish it with a rough rag. If a likely stump is not around, you may whittle down a crotched stick into a spoon or select a small burl and cut it from the tree, taking a longer

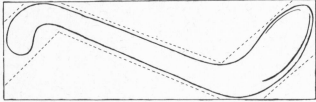

Spoon from a stump

handle than when you cut the noggin.

For those near the seashore and by deep stream beds, clam shells do well in place of burls and tree stumps. Gather tablespoon size to larger shells and green sticks 8–9 inches (20–23cm) long. Bore two holes in one end of each shell using a knife point or a nail drill. Split each stick at one end and bind it at the end of the break to keep it from splitting further. Bore corresponding holes in the split end of each stick, insert the shell and thread and bind the two together with hemp or milkweed fiber.

A clam shell spoon
for soups and stews

Forks: To finish setting the table, make some hardwood forks. Select young shoots with one or two crotches and cut them to allow for an 8-inch (20.0cm) handle. Trim the branches to make even tines and sharpen them with your knife.

K.P.

After each meal—inside or out—comes cleanup duty. Water and sand do a good scouring job, but to boost cleanliness make a rush brush from the horsetail plant. Look for a 15-inch (38cm) tall, green stalked plant with branches projecting from the sides. (The immature plant has a long, pink-stemmed stalk with a spore head at the top.) Gather a handful of the stalks and tie them together tightly with a length of cord or vine. Trim the top and the bottom evenly and hold it in your closed fist to scour the pot clean.

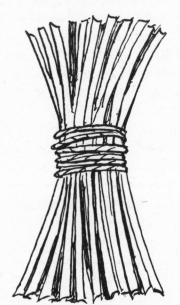

Horsetail plant
and rush brush

Brushes and Brooms: If you get carried away in cleaning up around camp, you will want to make a tent brush of long, thin, green willow, ash, or hemlock twigs. Cut a stout stick of the same wood and notch it at one end. Gather the collected sticks around the notch and bind them with basswood or other available fiber. You may even bore a hole in the handle, loop a thong through it, and hang it in the tent for fast "neat'ning up."

Plains Indian two-purpose brush

Another such broom once was made by the Pueblo and Plains Indians of broom sedge or other stiff grasses. A 3-inch (7cm) bundle of grasses was bound with a cord 4 inches (10cm) from one end. The grasses were trimmed evenly at both ends. The long straws were used to brush the dirt from floors, the short end served as a hair brush.

The Navajo made a combination hair and clothes brush from their natural resource, the yucca. After soaking and pounding the yucca fibers to remove the vegetable pulp, they bunched and tied them together in much the same way as the Plains and Pueblo Indians did the grasses.

The Latrine

Getting down to basics, your home in the woods needs a bathroom. Common sense shall dictate proximity to sleeping quarters, kitchen, and drinking water. Over a hole or a trench you can build a simple but sturdy

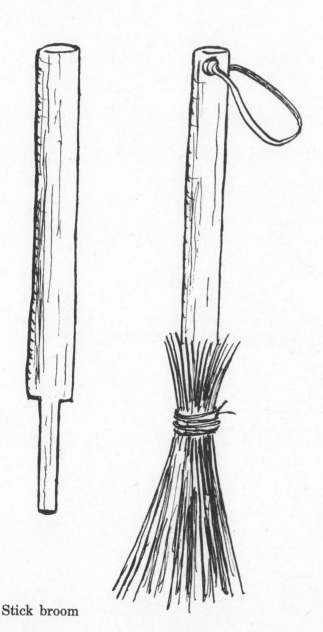

Stick broom

bench. Drive two strong and pointed stakes into the ground angling them backward. Near the bottom, cross these stakes with two others shorter than the first. Lash a knee-hold bar to the ends of the second set of braces and a back bar at the top of the long ones. Nearby, set a pointed spike into the ground—with a perpendicular fork to hold a roll of paper. To keep the audience at a minimum, you may frame the area with a tarp mounted to posts staked around the trench.

If you are there to "set a spell" and the Sears' catalog is nowhere in sight, a magazine rack might be a good wood w.c. addition.

Cut two 1-foot (.3m) high stakes and three or four sticks about half that size. Bore holes in the stakes at matching intervals, and sharpen the smaller branches to a rounded point at each end to fit the holes. Push the stakes into the ground near the paper post, and lay a few old periodicals over the sticks.

Outside the tarp, a washstand is readily constructed using three sticks lashed together a foot from the top. Set a bowl of water in the stand above the lashing, and if you have found one long branch with an offshoot to use in the tripod, you have a built-in towel rack, too.

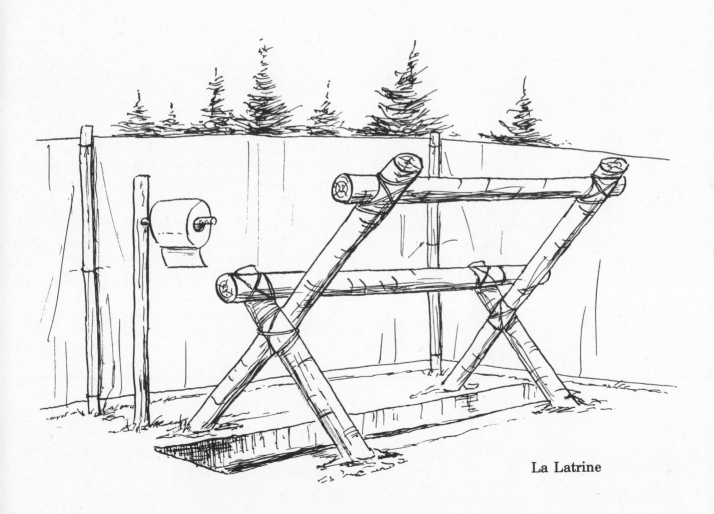

La Latrine

La Library

A shaving stand

A handy tree stump may also serve as an outdoor vanity or shaving stand. Cut head-high poles with forks and set them into the ground on either side and a little behind a convenient stump. Rest or lash a cross pole between the forks and hang a towel and washcloth from it. Set a wash bowl on the stump. If the framing poles have other handy projections, you may hang a mirror and even a cup with toothbrushes and tooth-paste in it from another. (If a toothbrush was

A tri-pod washstand

left off your list of camping gear, you can make one by simply chewing the end of a small green twig to a pulp and pounding the tip with a stone. Soap, salt, and baking soda are adequate substitutes for toothpaste.)

But a word of caution before you put wild growing shrubs to your mouth. A tiny sampling should allow you to detect an almond or bitter taste indicative of high acid content. These are almost sure danger signs of poison. Another indication of noxious elements is the color of the plant's sap. Red, black, or white sap oozing from trees or plants indicates danger if ingested. To be safe, never ingest or put into your mouth any part of a tree, plant, or shrub which you cannot identify.

Furnishings

Once the house is raised and the kettle is on, you can begin to plan additional camp furnishings. To make yourself at home, you can hang your hat, coat, and pack on a handy tree peg. Using your hatchet, make a vertical cut into a neighboring tree. Drive a pointed wooden peg into it and mount your hang-ups there. Remember to remove the peg when you leave. The tree will heal itself. Cutting a dual-branched stick stub in half (as shown), you can make two clothes hooks at once. They are attached to the tree with lashings, thereby not injuring it in any way.

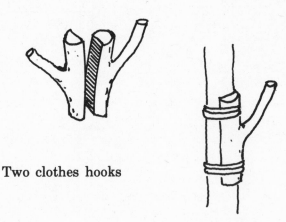

Two clothes hooks

Lashing a clothes hook to a tree

Seating: Camp stools are easy to make and are usually the camp's first furniture. Split in two a fallen log about 1 foot (.3m) long. Shave or sand one side flat and smooth. With an auger or your jackknife, bore four leg holes in the rounded bark side. Now, cut four seasoned hardwood branches 20 inches (50cm) long and 1½–2 inches (4–5cm) in diameter, and trim one end of each to fit a peg hole. Split the whittled end and insert it in the bored hole. You may glue the legs into the base or wedge them in more securely with small pieces of hardwood. A full bench may be made in the same fashion using a longer split of log. If you like a back rest, one may be easily turned out by cutting poles of

Wherever you hang your hat is home.

Simple camp stool

equal length and mounting them in bored holes near the back of the flat seat. Mount and lash one or more horizontal cross poles to form a back rest. Add a couple of grass-filled old pillow cases, and you have a couch with cushions!

In 10–15 minutes, you can even come up with a full chair. Locate two strong, forked sticks about 4 feet (1.2m) long and 3 inches (7.5cm) thick, one of which has a prong 9–10 inches (23–25cm) long and the other with a prong of 12–15 inches (30–38cm). A third stout branch with a fork at one end is set into the ground with the other branches propped and lashed to it. Using 1-inch (2.5cm) thick smooth sticks, make a seat and back by lashing them to the prongs and to the main branch. Have a sit down, a rest, and a cup of tea.

Forest fork chair (improvised)

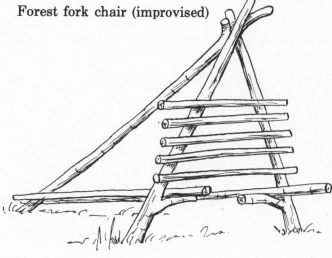

Forest fork chair

If such unique pronged branches aren't readily available, you can still make a seat. Find two sticks about 3½ feet (1m) long with small forks—stilt-like footholds—about 8 inches (20cm) from one end. Brace these into a 4-foot (1.2m) long forked pole, lay 5-foot (1.5m) long poles from the small forks near the bottom, and lash them together and to the back frame. Now, lay seating and back sticks as you did for the first chair. Set your chair in front of a foot-stool stump and wait for the call of the wild.

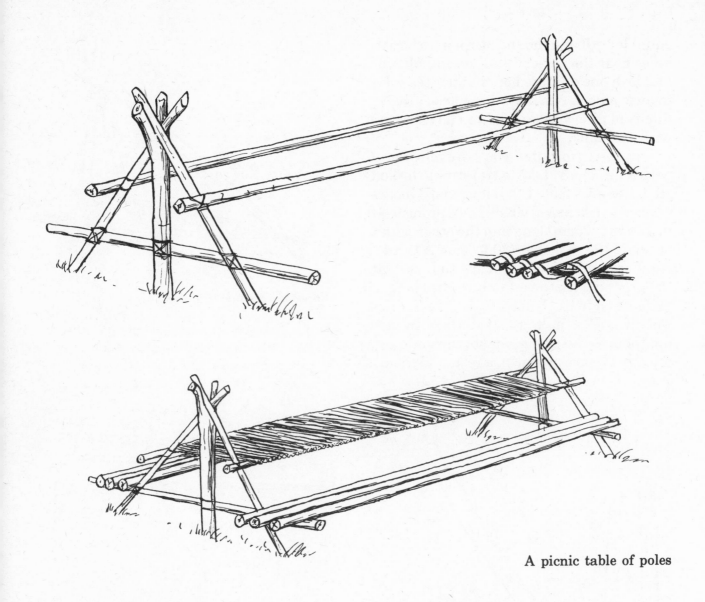

A picnic table of poles

Picnic Table: Although most campers are used to balancing a plate in one hand, a cup in another, and raking the fire with a third, a table can easily be made to accommodate four to five persons for "formal" outdoor eating. To frame the table, set two forked stakes 3 inches (7.5cm) thick and 5 feet (1.5m) long about 1½–2 feet (.45–.6m) into the ground with the fork prong outward. The two stakes should be 5-7 feet (1.5–2m) apart. Cut four strong, straight poles 4½–5 feet (1.35–1.5m) long and 2 inches (5cm) thick. Notch, cross, and set two in each crotch of the set poles. Lash a cross pole 2 feet (.6m) from the ground to each of the two bracing sets and lash table length poles to the side poles at eating level. Lash straight and equally long sticks together—eight to the foot—and to the table top poles. Finally, lay three 3- to 4-inch (7.5–10cm) thick and 6-foot (1.8m) long poles on the bracing stakes as seats. Do not lash them, but leave them free for adjusting for comfortable seating.

A two-tree table is readily constructed

The table is just large enough for one place setting. Larger tables can be made by adjusting the dimensions proportionally.

between adjacent trees by lashing a strong pole to either side of the trees. Cut several poles a bit longer than the table width and tie them across the main poles. The same table can be made using only one tree. Frame the tree with the two stout poles and lash cross sticks to it (as illustrated on the cover). Make sure that these are sturdily constructed if you intend to rest containers of hot foods or liquid on these wooden ledges.

Compass Clock: Outdoors your stomach usually dictates when you eat, but if you are a clock watcher and want to know the time, why not construct a clock compass in a sunny spot of your campsite? One starry night, locate the North Star by raising your eyes from the outer lip of the Big Dipper to a star at the end of the Little Dipper's handle. The North Star is in a straight line between the two. On a level spot of ground where the sun shines constantly during the day, drive an 8- to 10-foot (2.4–3m) stake into the ground at a 45-degree angle pointing at the star. Next noon when the sun is at its zenith, set a small stake at the far end of the shadow made by the larger one. Then set 10 more stakes equidistant from one another. It is as accurate as you will need in the woods. Of course, calibration with a watch or clock will add considerable accuracy to this device.

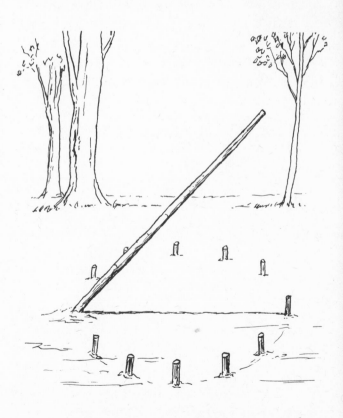

To tell time by day start with the stars.

Light: Campfire light is lovely for singing and storytelling, but it is necessarily stationary. There are times when you will want a smaller light in the tent or on the table at an after-dark dinner. The following are alternative light sources.

Mud lamp—Half fill a coffee or other can with mud. Splinter several flammable sticks and wrap them together with a spiral of twisted cloth; set them in the mud and allow it to dry. Fill the can to just below the top with bacon or other melted fat and light the sticks. Inside, this light provides heat, illumination, and a little smoke.

Germ lamp—If you have time to wait for this one, a germ lamp can add an interesting glow to any tent or hut. Cook up a bit of beef boullion and add enough powdered gelatin to allow it to harden as it cools. Add glowing wood chips to the just warm jell-soup, stir, and pour the whole thing into a glass jar. Set it aside for about three weeks. At the end of that time the bacteria will give off enough light to keep the pitch dark at bay.

A birch bark torch

Torches are good portable lights for getting from bed to latrine and back or for lighting the chess board on the table after dinner.

Birch provides a sure torch light. Just coil an 18-inch (45cm) length of bark to a thickness of 2 inches (5cm). Bind it up with string if necessary. Split the end of a green stick and insert the bark. Light it and hold it aloft to shine on your table or path. The same effect can be gained from a pine knot or a cattail soaked in melted fat.

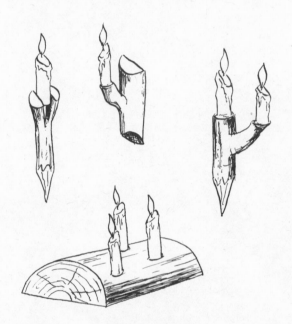

Improvised holders for commercial candles

Candles—If you have a corner of your backpack to spare and can squeeze in a few utility candles, so much the better. You may make holders out of various solid and scrap woods. Returning to the do-all peg which is whittled to a point at one end, you need only split the other and insert the candle. Or you may whittle out a hollow for the candle in the peg top. A half slice of log makes a good mount for any number of candles. Bore staggered holes along its length or vary the depth of the holes and you have something with a bit more style.

Camp "Carpeting": Depending on what size you make these cat mats, you can have place mats for your table or rugs for your earthen floor. Gather cattail rushes and dry them. Briefly water soak them to make them pliable and braid them in threes adding another as one begins to taper. Coil the braids in concentric circles, using fine cording to hold the rug or place mat together. Stop anywhere you like from coaster-size to wall-to-wall splendor.

Lashed ladder

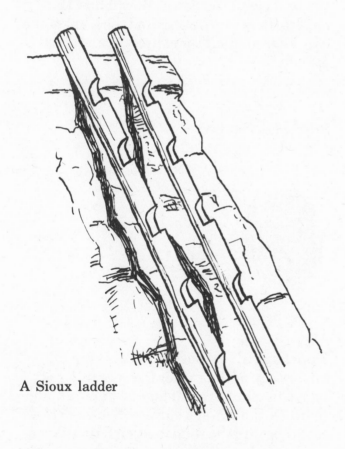

A Sioux ladder

Ladder: A last bit of furniture can be a handy item in or out of camp. To make a ladder such as the Sioux and other Indians used, simply cut two stout poles of close-to-even length and cut notches in one side of each. Set them 1 foot (.3m) apart and at a 45-degree angle to the wall or tree you are climbing. Another variety is made by lash-ing two fallen saplings together at their tapered ends and spreading the bottoms 2½–3 feet (.75–.94m) apart and tightly lashing stick rungs between the poles.

Catching Dinner

With home and hearth constructed for a stay, it is time to go fishing—for relaxation and for dinner. Spur-of-the-moment preparations are easy.

Hooks: Make your own hooks of half-finger (diameter) size sticks with wood slivers lashed upward from the bottom. Increase your luck by lashing several splinters

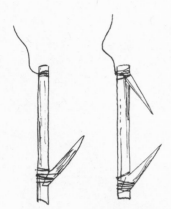

Wood splinter fish hooks

upright or adding one pointing down from the top.

Spear: If you feel like a night out and want to get right into the direct act of fishing, make yourself a fishing spear. Cut 6 to 8 hardwood sticks 2–3 feet (.6–.9m) long, and shape the end of each into a point. Cluster the sticks, and lash them together about a foot (.3m) above the points. The intent is not to pierce the fish with the spear but to pin it down. Working at night with a torch in the sandy shallows of a stream, move slowly, strike quickly, and dinner is as good as in the pan.

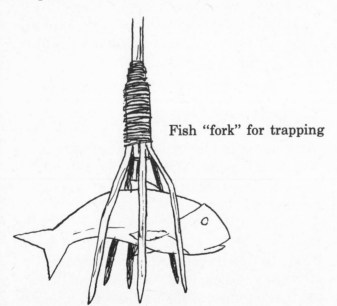

Fish "fork" for trapping

Log Trap: Based on the fact that fish only swim forward, the hollow log trap is a good way to catch a meal for those who would rather be off doing something else *while* fishing. Pick a hollow log which is not too large in diameter and cover one end with a woven net of vines or cord. Tie a rope sling around the log nearest the open end, insert a bit of spoiled fish or meat about 2 to 3 inches (5–7.5cm) inside the opening, and lower the log into the pool. With the open end upstream, you will catch the fish as they follow the natural flow of the water and the scent of the bait. Merely haul them up, out, and on to dinner.

Hollow log fish trap

Fish Corral: Another form of trap takes advantage of the rather low mentality of fish. Cut a quantity of logs just long enough to break the water's surface. Set them close together into the sand in a pen formation, as illustrated, with the opening upstream. The fish will swim in easily but will only find their way out by default.

Fishing Floats: To improve the odds over one pole, line, and hook, set a mess of stick floats adrift in calm water. Cut straight branches 2 feet (.6m) long and, using thong, cord, or strips of bark, lash a heavy stone to

Fish corral

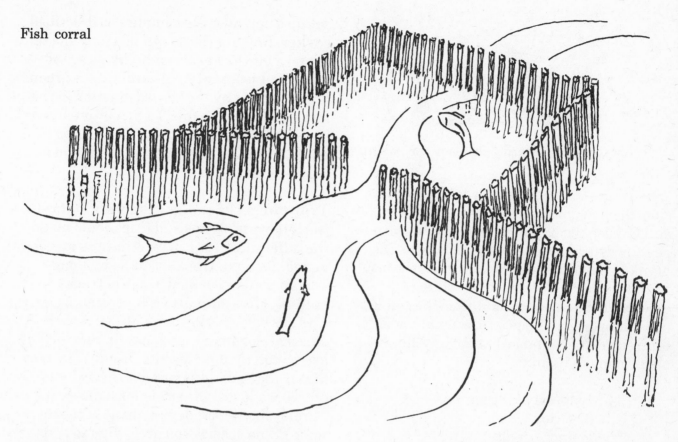

one end to keep the stick upright in the water. Attach a line 2–3 yards (2–3m) long to the top of each stick and bait a thorn or splinter hook with decomposing meat or other favorite bait. Set the sticks into the water, noting the current and the wind so you will be able to find them again when you

return several hours later. If fishing from the shore is what you are there for, a corn cob bobber works well to keep track of bites and nibbles.

Corn cob bobber

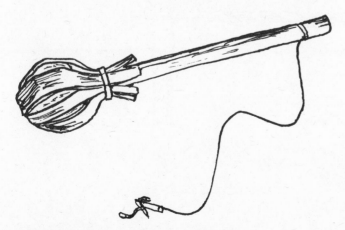

Weighted stick for absentee fishing

Menu: Back at camp, the menu calls for fresh planked fish. Cut a flat piece of 3-inch (7.5cm) thick hardwood somewhat longer than the fish. Bore four or five holes in the plank and sharpen small wooden pegs to fit them. Propping the plank on a log, pre-heat

Planked and pegged fish ready for baking

it in the glow of reflecting fire. Meanwhile, split the fish down the back and spread it out. Grease the hot plank and spread and peg the fish, skin-side down, on it. Prop the plank before the fire again and cook the fish until it is flaky. To keep it hot while you enjoy your catch, eat it right from the plank.

Camp bread is a good accompaniment for fresh fish . . . and just about anything else. To make it, mix:

> 1 tsp. of baking powder
> 6 oz. flour
> a pinch of salt
> water or milk

Knead into a tough dough. (The ingredients can be brought from home in a clean cloth or packed in a coffee can.) To bake the bread,

set up a spit over the campfire as described earlier. Roll out the dough in a long snake shape a bit thicker than thumb-size, and wrap it at loose intervals around the green branch spit. Lay the "breaded" stick in the forks and over the fire. Turn it often to bake it evenly. To check for doneness insert a thin stick. When it comes out dry, the bread is ready to eat.

Trapping: For on-land hunters for food, the following snares and traps could mean the difference between meeting and missing a meal. Animal traps are best set along known trails, so a knowledge of tracks is helpful. Most animals will respond to fish or meat as bait, but lay out a larder of carrots, oatmeal, cornmeal, or leafy vegetables if you are trying to catch rabbits. Handle the trap materials as little as possible, and when you do, wear gloves. Other means to mask the human smell include fire, urine of the female of the species you are trying to trap, and salt.

The box trap works well for small game such as squirrels and rabbits. To make it, set a box on the ground with one side precariously resting on a small stick which in turn

Camp bread-kabob

Box trap for small mammals

is resting on a flat rock. Attach a string to the stick and conceal the string with leaves and dirt. Set your bait deep inside the box, and conceal yourself some yards away in the underbrush. When the animal enters the trap, jerk the stick and the box will fall, trapping the animal inside. To set up the box trap for your absence, rest the bait on a small piece of wood at the back of the box and run the string from the top of the main pole to it. When the animal moves the food, and subsequently the wood, the stick will fall, and it will be trapped.

Deadfall: Set a forked stick into the ground. Notch it slightly about half way down. Sharpen a stick of equal diameter at one end and pierce a piece of bait with it. Set a notch near the other end of the bait stick. Cut another stick to act as a log prop and assemble the notched pieces in a triangular numeral "4" as illustrated. Prop a large log at the peak of the contraption. As the prey attempts to remove the bait, the precarious

assembly is disturbed and the set log falls on the animal. A large log will kill the prey instantly.

Trapping Rules: Trapping is best practiced as a last means for survival and only then by following these rules:

1. Set your trap safely so it will not surprise and injure anyone.
2. Post written warnings in the area.
3. Do not leave your trap and forget it; an animal might needlessly suffer or a person may stumble on it long after your signs have disappeared.
4. Be aware of local game laws and conservation regulations.

Moving On

The fact that you are out in the woods to live for a week or a light year is indicative of the American syndrome of restlessness. Roots are replantable. If you get the urge to see what is over the next hill or on the other side of the glade, the following items should help transport that which is not tied down or cannot be easily replaced when you set foot in a new spot.

Baskets and Backpacks: Using the weaving method described earlier, you can make a basket backpack 18 inches (45cm) square at the opening and 2–2½ feet (.65m) deep. The material should be cane, rushes, or whatever pliable but sturdy grasses are available. The straps are also woven long enough to work your arms and shoulders in. They are attached at the top of the pannier and 18 inches (45cm) down.

A brace to make the load rest easier as you lug it along can be constructed using two bent ash sticks fastened at right angles to one another. Fill in the blank spaces

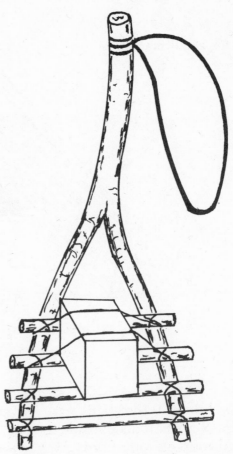

Moving on? Make a litter.

A catch-all and carry-all pannier

between them with rawhide, and brace the frame using thong hinges. Fashion arm loops with long thongs.

Litter: If you have more than a backpack can carry, you might consider making an outdoor "U-haul," a litter for dragging behind you as you transplant yourself in the woods. Find a forked tree branch and cut it so there are 4 feet (1.2m) above the fork joint and 2 straight feet (.6m) below. An 8-inch (20.0cm) diameter branch will make a sturdy brace. Lay the branch on the ground and cross the fork with several sticks and lash them down. Knot a rope to the end of the litter's "arm" and you are ready to move.

Being at home in the woods is a matter of approach, meeting the challenge of making do, and not regretting the kitchen sink and other comforts of modern living left behind. It takes practice for some and comes naturally to others. It has its own and many rewards.

Need a lift? Love a tree.

6

The Forest Afloat

Swim, float, or go by boat. These are the options you face when there is no way of getting 'round a river, stream, or small lake that sets itself in your path. Read on before you wade in.

Buoyed Bedding

The first means of getting to the other side of the water is recommended for campers and hikers who have little gear. Wrap all your belongings, including your hiking boots, in the center of a ground cover, tying the corners and folds together tightly so as not to allow water to seep in. To boost the water tightness, layer fern, grass, or brush on the ground sheet before filling it with your gear and tying it. Tie a cord to the pack and to a belt loop so that if it should get away from you, you can reel it back in and float on. If you are traveling in a party of people, tie two ground sheet buoys together for added support.

Tarp Raft

Three or more ground sheets stuffed with available grasses and lashed together can make a sturdy raft for transporting party and parcels across or along a stream. Lay each ground sheet flat on the ground. Cut lengths of grasses or light brush (two-thirds as long as the ground sheet) and bundle them into bolster shapes. Lay a brush bolster in the center of each ground sheet, wrap, and tie water tight. Lash three or four together with cording, and secure the whole with a smooth stick on the top at either end to lend support for your load.

Birch Bark Canoe

The first Americans built the original 9- to 20-foot (2.7-6.0m) birch bark canoes for hunting, trading, and war. After the Indians, hunters, explorers, and lumberjacks adopted the craft. Then the canoe was turned over to the tourists. The first canoe tourist in Maine was Henry David Thoreau, who made two canoes of his own to explore the woods and waters in the 1850s.

Maine was only a fraction of the 1,000-mile-wide swath from which the Indians selected birch for their canoes. The area extended from New York City to Hudson Bay and west and northwest to the Pacific. The biggest and best birch trees for canoes are now found in New Brunswick, Nova Scotia, Maine, Quebec, and parts of Ontario.

Besides birch, the Indians made canoes from the bark of elm, hickory, spruce, basswood, and chestnut trees. These, however, are inferior to birch because they absorb water and become waterlogged and heavy. Other bark canoes often were made on one side of the stream, used to cross over and

discarded on the other side. With careful maintenance, the birch bark canoes could last as long as 10 years.

The construction of the birch bark canoe begins, of course, with the selection of the right tree. It should be absolutely straight or else the bark will pucker as it is worked, and it should be free of branches and knotholes. Although few canoes are made of a single piece of bark, the builder will choose a tree with as long a portion of unbroken line as possible. A sample is cut near the base of the tree and is bent to determine its elasticity. (When it breaks, the best bark will not separate into layers.) By just looking at the tree bark, a skillful canoe builder can tell whether a sturdy vessel can be made from it. If the eyes—the dotted lines running in the direction of the grain—are close together, the bark will be weak and unfit for river'

Spring bark ready for removing

Chiseling birch bark with flat-end poles

Drying bark . . . carefully!

crossings.

Most bark is selected in the spring or early summer, when the sap is up and it comes away easily from the green tree. Sometime during the winter, make two cuts down the length of the tree on opposite sides and two circular cuts top and bottom. In the spring, you simply lift the bark from the tree. Another form of removal is accomplished using only one vertical cut in a zig-zag line and two circular cuts at the top and bottom, according to the length of bark needed. Two long poles are whittled flat at one end each, then crossed and inserted into the vertical cut in the bark. Working up and down, the bark virtually is chiseled from the tree.

The bark is then rolled brown-side-out and against the length, tied with a pine root, cord, or spruce or cedar bark thong, and carried to the building bed. If the bark threatens to crack and break, it has to be worked to be made pliable. One way to do

this is to build a small, quick fire of leaves and spread the bark over it open side down. Of course, this operation has to be tended carefully so as not to lose the fledgling canoe in a blaze.

Bark canoes are built on open ground 20 feet (6m) long and free of rocks and roots which might cause punctures. Ribs are made of cedar cut into 4- to 5-foot (1.2–1.5m) lengths and ⅜-inch (9mm) thicknesses, the center ribs being 2–2½ inches (5–6cm) wide but tapered to 1–1½ inches (2.5–3.75cm) toward the ends of the canoe. The cedar lengths are rounded on the edges and tapered with a crooked knife, tied together into two-part sets and soaked over a day's time to make them pliable for bending. The Indians, as do the few remaining bark canoe makers of today, judged much of their work by eye. Estimating the bottom width of the canoe, they marked and bent the ribs accordingly after first heating them with boiling water for several minutes. The bending was done by placing the rib sets on the ground, standing at the marks, and pulling the ribs up around the sides of the feet. The rib ends were then tied at the top to hold the bend. The sharper bends, those needed for the bow and stern, were done around a post, a sapling, or a raised knee.

Cedar also is used in the gunwales, those strips of wood that run along the top of each of the canoe's sides. The gunwales consist of an inwale and an outwale, the first being a strip of cedar squared in the center and tapered to the ends and the outwale being a thinner strip. The edge of the bark and the tips of the ribs are pinched between the gunwales and lashed with spliced roots.

If several pieces of bark are used to form the canoe, the construction obviously will result in some overlap. With the use of summer and winter barks, the result can be an attractive patchwork. The summer bark turns lighter and lighter brown until it reaches a high buff color. The brown, winter bark turns darker and darker. The overlap is always sewn so that the edge faces the stern of the canoe. This is done so that this weaker section will not tear open under the constant pressure of the water and so it will not catch on a rock or other obstruction which might jolt the canoe.

To make the canoe water tight, all seams are sealed with the pitch of white or black spruce which is tapped just as a maple tree is tapped to collect sap for syrup. The sap is boiled to thicken it and is used frequently to touch up spots which might let the water in. The Indians mixed animal fat with their spruce gum sealant so the bark seams would not crack in the cold weather. Today, asphalt works as well.

Rather than go into the intricate construction of a hand-crafted 10-year canoe (which might take a full summer to make), I will leave such detail to the experts. For step-by-step instruction on birch bark canoe building, see those works referred to in the Bibliography at the end of this book. Instead, the following will let you in on the simple secrets of makeshift canoe building for a short season's jaunt.

Once you have the bark selected, cut, and back at the campsite, proceed to flex it and ply it with hot water until it can be turned inside out. All bark canoes are con-

Tie ribs to hold form

A once-across-the water canoe

structed so that the side of the bark closest to the wood is the side which makes contact with the water. Draw the ends of the bark together lengthwise. Six to fifteen inches (15–37.5cm) from each end, mark and cut with your knife a staggered series of holes from the top to the bottom of the forming canoe. Lace them shut with vines or tough bark. (The Indians preferred the roots of the white spruce). To brace and waterproof the canoe ends stuff the inside of each with clay.

To keep the canoe open and serviceable, spreaders are needed. Cut two pieces of wood 2 feet (.6m) long and 4 inches (10cm) thick and notch the center of each. These are the spreader ends. Cut two sets of holes centered at the top of each side of the bark. Through these sets, spaced 18–20 inches (45–50cm) apart, the spreader ends are lashed to the canoe sides. The actual spreader is a strong stick which is cut long enough to keep the canoe open. It is inserted into the side notches of the lashed sticks.

Loading and Launching   The Indians loaded and launched their crafts in a foot (.3m) of water. This is a safe margin, given the fact you may not know what lies just below the surface. No canoe should be loaded so heavily with people and parcels that the gunwales will be any closer than 6 inches (15cm) to the waterline.

Poles, Paddles, and Paddling   Poling with a 12-foot (3.6m) long branch propels a canoe faster than paddling and is especially useful when going upstream. But the standard method of moving the craft through the water is by paddling it. The best paddles are made of sturdy, flexible maple with a medium wide (6 inches; 25cm) blade rounded almost to a point and with a pear-shaped grip. (The taper of the blade allows it to be used like a pole in shallow water although purists cringe at the thought. The paddle, cut on the straight of the grain, is roughed out with an ax and carved with a crooked knife. Its tip may just come to your chin as some prefer, or it may reach over your head. With good care it can last two to three years—if it does not grow feet and walk away as many do in populated areas. Your paddle should not be left in the sun to dry, nor laid on the ground where it may be stepped on. It is usually best to carry two for dual paddling or for use as a spare.

The proper paddling position in the bow and stern of a canoe is kneeling. This position lowers the center of gravity, adds stability, and sets the whole body to work, making the arms less likely to tire during power stroking. The Indians paddled with short, light, rapid chops which take less energy. Latterday canoeists tend to take longer and harder strokes.

The best stroke to keep the canoe on an even keel is accomplished with the paddle turned outward, away from the boat, at the end of a "J" shaped stroke. It counters the boat's tendency to turn in the opposite direction. Perhaps a bit easier is a stroke which ends with the paddle flat against the side of the canoe and astern (behind) the paddler. In this way the paddle acts as a rudder to control the direction of the canoe. When two are in a canoe, one in the bow and the other in the stern, each paddles on an opposite side with equal strength and length of stroke. This helps to keep the canoe "right on." (In this case, the stern paddler actually steers and the man or woman in the bow adds muscle to propel the boat in a straight line.)

Like riding a bike, this skill must be learned by doing. Versatility is a key to good canoeing, so learn to paddle well on both sides. Safety is especially important in a canoe, since once you have capsized you must make it ashore before setting off again. The following are a few points to absorb as second nature:

Canoe with sail set

1. Enter and exit a canoe holding both gunwales.

2. Plant your legs firmly against the inside walls of the canoe.

3. Do not make any sudden moves without informing your paddling partner so that he or she can compensate and keep the canoe stable.

4. Do not load the canoe so that the gunwale is less than 6 inches (15cm) above the water.

5. Always wear a life jacket.

6. Use a canoe buddy-system in difficult waters.

7. If you turn over, hold on to the canoe until help arrives.

8. Never solo canoe in water which is less than 50 degrees F. (10°C).

9. Pack all small gear in waterproof bags and tie them to the thwarts (braces across the canoe). Pack other gear in duffle bags, but leave them loose in the canoe bottom.

10. Canoe in water that matches your skill level.

11. Watch out for fallen or floating trees, low bridges, or overhead branches, and lean forward to duck under obstacles. If you lean backward you may swamp the boat.

12. If the canoe is moving fast do not hold onto anything stationary.

13. Stay away from dams.

14. If the canoe gets caught up on a rock or other obstacle in the river or stream, let it swing around in the current to free itself.

15. On large bodies of water, paddle close to the shore.

Sailing   Why waste a good wind paddling when you can harness it and sail? Using the two paddles as masts, lash a polyethylene or nylon ground cloth to them; then hoist and hold them vertically. The Indians used sheets of bark or even moose hide as sails or set a leafy bush in the bow of the canoe to take advantage of a good breeze.

Today, bark canoe building is all but an abandoned art. There are, according to John McPhee in *The Survival of the Bark Canoe,* only three or four Indians in Canada, an old man in Minnesota, and Henry Vaillancourt in New Hampshire whose passion and skill persist. Nearly gone, but not yet forgotten.

Coracle

The coracle is another water transport vehicle which utilizes the handy canvas, heavy duck tarp, or ground cover. To construct a coracle, first measure your tarp and subtract 18 inches (45.0cm) from each side to allow for turning up the sides of the boat. Draw an oval shape on open ground to the adjusted dimension and draw another oval about 9 inches (22.5cm) inside the first. Cut a quantity of sticks 2 feet (.6m) long and sharpened at one end. Set the points down into the ground 6–8 inches (15–20cm) apart along both oval lines. This is the frame for your coracle stuffing. Gather branches, dead fern or bush material and loosely pack it between the frame ribs to about 15 inches (38cm) in height. Bind the filler material with vines, bark strips, or other cording material. To brace the bottom, cut several sticks a bit shorter than the full length of the coracle and lash them across the top of the oval grass form. Cross these sticks with others and lash widthwise.

Lay the tarp flat on the ground next to the filler structure and cover the center with 6 inches (15.0cm) of loose fern, grass, or light branch padding. Carefully lifting the filler form straight up from its stick frame, turn it over and lay it in the center (on the diagonal) of the readied tarp. Turn up the sides of the tarp and lash them to the floor frame.

An 8 × 10 foot (2.4–3.0m) tarp will make a coracle suitable for carrying three to four people. Each person should ride sitting upright, neither pressing against nor sitting on the side walls, which can easily break down and allow water to leak into the boat. The coracle can be propelled with a pole, a paddle, or a set of oars lashed to the top of the side walls. At night, the coracle skin reverts to lean-to, groundcover or other campsite cloth.

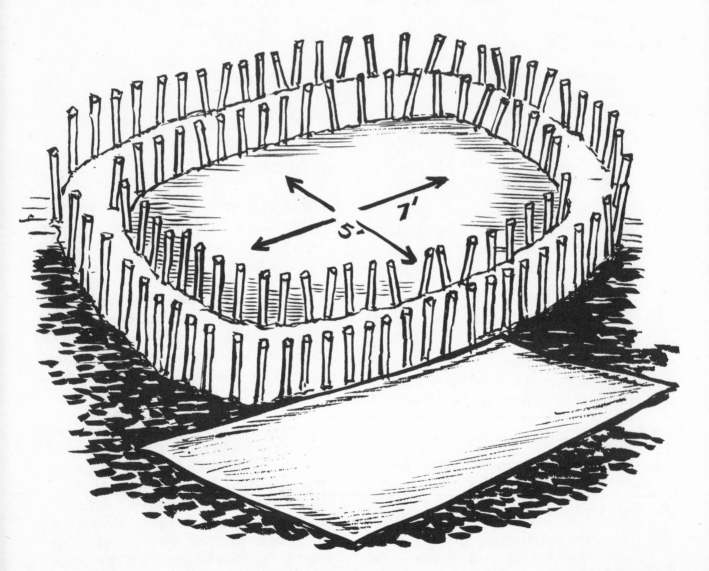

Coracle frame

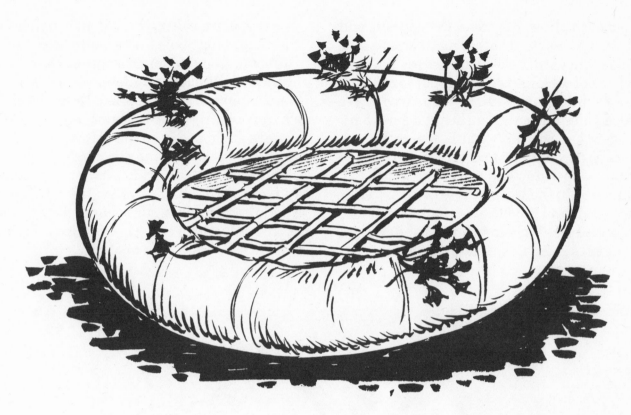

Coracle ready for launching

Raft

If rafts can be made by legendary Missouri boys to float on the Mississippi, they can be constructed readily by wilderness wanderers as the need arises. A three-log raft may be sufficient for a one-person party, but for a larger number the resulting craft should be about 12 feet (3.6m) long and 6 feet (1.8m) wide. Cut the quantity of 12–14 inch (30–35cm) logs accordingly. All main logs should be well matched in size so the raft will be level. If you build your raft on top of two logs (smooth on one side and aimed down the water's embankment) your launch will be more easily accomplished. Notch a main log at one end with broad based notches, one above and one below and offset

Notch logs evenly for assembly

from each other. Repeat at the opposite end. Mark and notch the other main logs so that the notches will be even across the top and bottom of all logs. Choosing four logs of narrower diameter, whittle them into three-sided poles and cut them about a foot (.3m) longer than the raft's width. Insert the wedges through the four sets of main log notches, two atop and two below. When launched in the water, these cross pieces will swell and bind the raft together. If the fit is too loose for comfort, inset thin wood wedges to swell and tighten the joints.

If you are rafting in still and shallow water, you may pole along using an 8- to 10-foot (2.4–3.0m) long smoothed tree branch of sufficient diameter so as not to bend when weight is applied. In rapids or when traveling down stream, you will need a shore anchor to keep the raft straight and steady. This anchor may be a large rock or a heavy log tied to the raft with long cording and laid on the shore. To steer the raft, make a paddle from a long curved branch flattened at the wide, thick end. Use it in front of the raft rather than at the back.

Poling is a primary means to keep a raft moving

Outrigger

The Papuans of New Guinea and other Pacific islanders construct a single-arm outrigger with a platform spanning the narrow central piece of a dugout canoe and with a cloth canopy to protect them from the tropical sun. You may go "luxury" or pop for the simpler kind called the "waterflea." A woodland trimaran consists of a fallen tree trunk whittled at each end into a sharp point. Cross the log with a long pole just in back of the front end and again near the back. Cut two smaller diameter logs and whittle their ends into points. Lash these logs parallel to the main rig at the ends of the poles. Finally, lash two smaller logs on either side of the main one. When you straddle the log in the center to ride the rig, these logs will act as foot rests as you paddle along.

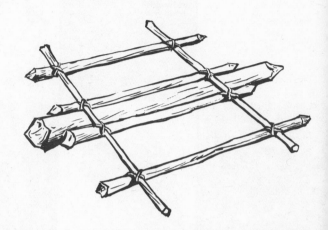

Outrigger; the fastest forest afloat

Wilderness Art Constructions, Toys and Games

The art of construction is making something special out of the nothing under other people's feet, silk purses from sows' ears if you like. A construction may be made only of found wood or be a combination of forest finds and sought out accompaniments. A subject for your *object d'art* may evolve from the first piece picked up, one suggesting a theme, a title, a feeling, or an abstract thought. As you walk in the woods, other pieces will jump to view and be compared to the first. They will either fit, be discarded, or suggest a work of their own.

Your own taste will determine what you pick up—that and how far you must carry the wood back to the house, the campsite, or the car. You may begin your selection by looking for pieces which suggest a recognizable object or those which simply offer interesting studies in shape and texture. Other

forest finds such as nuts, seeds, moss, pods, feathers, vine strands, and bark and the waterside treasures of shells, fish hooks, and reeds are marvelous additions that change the tempo and texture of a work. It may be just such a seemingly out-of-place object that transforms the obscure and unrelated into art.

Where to look is where you are—anywhere and everywhere. At the water's edge, in the forest, the desert, the mountains, and in the open fields. Certain times of the year are better than others, however, as the movements of the earth and the changing seasons bring pieces to the surface and the shores. Look near lakes in the spring and near the oceans in the fall and spring. Search for light, bleached-gray wood in the desert and darker grained pieces in the mountains from July through September. In the fields you will find all manner of dried twigs, branches, and broken stumps. All tell a tale as vignettes, parts of a lost whole, and offer their episodic remains for use in a new creation.

The woods you select should be dry and non-rotting. Wood which has a silver patina is well-aged. Pick up common shapes as well as the unusual. Always have a supply of straight, curved, and common block shapes on hand. The gear for getting all of your supplies should include a canvas shoulder bag to carry home found objects, a saw to cut small dead pieces from larger ones, and a pair of gloves for scrounging in depth.

Purists use what they find as they find it, refusing to change a knob or wart of the original piece. Others disdain nature's virtue, and carve as they see fit, highlighting a strong feature or bringing out a hidden highlight with the deft stroke of a knife. Whichever type of constructionist you become, you will at least want to clean the soil and resident creatures out of your wood before bringing it into your house. Silt and clinging dirt may be flushed out with water with or without detergent. You may use an old toothbrush to work in the crevices. To remove bark and sap, use wet sand or scrape it away. (See Chapter 2 under "Curing" for additional procedures to remove sap.)

The ideal result is a clean, dry piece of wood in prime condition. The following method works best to preserve the original find. Spread out your pieces in an area with good ventilation. Turn them frequently to dry evenly and to reduce the risk of cracking. The longer the wood dries the better. Do not be in a rush. If you have pieces of wood both in process and complete, you will always have new forms from which to choose.

To achieve that "silver fox" patina, the wood should be weathered outside in the sun, rain, and wind. This can be achieved naturally in about a week if the weather cooperates, or urged along by soaking the pieces in a 50–50 solution of water and household bleach. For special effects, you may brush the wood with undiluted bleach. This results in a yellow-brown color. Or you may use commercial wood bleach for a plaster white finish.

To accent the natural beauty of the wood, many wood constructionists rub the surface with the tip of a deerhorn. This compresses the fibers of the wood and adds a soft sheen. It is possible to accent only certain areas, if you do not wish to highlight the entire piece of wood. Deerhorns are available through jewelry and bead supply stores.

Other finishes can be created using shoe polish, floor or car wax, or the special wax developed for drift- and found-wood artists. The wax is applied with the hands. This is called French polishing and adds a very warm luster to the wood. The piece may be buffed with a clean cloth or brush afterward. This wax and other wood constructionist materials are available through: Drift House, 4337 Cottage Way, Sacramento, CA 95825.

Color, too, may be added to make something new from old wood. Oil, acrylics, household latex, and wood stains are all good. In order not to lose the interesting grain of your piece, you can make a transparent stain. Art oils can be thinned with turpentine and acrylics, and other water-based paints may be mixed 50–50 with water before applying. To seal the painted wood, you may use a matte or gloss media or other sealants available in art stores.

Bases

Just as framing an art print or painted picture can enhance or detract from it, so the base on which you mount your wood construction is important to its final appearance. You may use found boards, flat or rounded, with or without knots or holes. These, too, should be dry and non-rotting. The best mounts become a part of the art itself.

If no found wood is large enough to serve as a mount, you may substitute painted masonite. Cut a masonite board to the size you need and frame it in pine, painting or staining it to finish. Cut a piece of Styrofoam to fit and press and glue the pieces into it. The Styrofoam may be camouflaged with florist materials resembling natural fern, moss, etc.

Box assemblage is a cousin to relief construction. Boxes are their own frames. You can make an assemblage in an individual box or combine several for a single artistic statement. Cigar boxes, when they can be found, are good construction boxes. You may set them on a table, to be opened naturally, or you may hinge two together and stand them up like open books.

For the constructions described so far, you have needed little more than an eye for the find and fingers for putting it all together. Avid constructionists have a full craft shop at hand. From the following list of tools, you may choose what you will need right now, adding others when and as you wish:

hacksaw	screwdriver
coping saw	compass
hand drill	sandpaper
scissors	lids, jar tops, and cans
straight edge	pliers
ratchet braces	nails and screws
auger bits	hammer
mat knife	wire
wood vise	tacks

A hammer and nails, wood dowels, and glue are the basics for holding wood constructions together. White glue works well in wood-to-wood construction; epoxy is recommended for pieces that will be hung outdoors. The following are common construction combinations and their suggested adhesives:

Wood to wood—white, resin, plastic resin urea base, and waterproof glues.

Plastic to wood—white, resin, plastic resin urea base, waterproof glues, and contact cement.

Wood outdoors—plastic resin urea base, waterproof glues, and contact cement.

Metal to wood—white or resin glue, epoxy, epoxy metal, or contact cement.

Cloth to wood—white, resin, or household glue, or polymer medium.

Leather to wood—white or resin glue, polymer medium, or contact cement.

Rubber to wood—epoxy, epoxy metal, or contact cement, household glue.

Stone or concrete to wood—epoxy cement.

For best results when gluing dissimilar materials together, you should determine which are porous (cloth, paper, cardboard, brick, wood, leather) and which are nonporous (glass, metal, china, plastics, rubber), and use the adhesive suggested for the nonporous material.

Wood as "Canvas"

Painting on wood has become popular among nature-loving artists. Squirrels, woodpeckers, and even whole woodland scenes are being painted straight onto bark and other rough wood pieces. The texture and irregularity of the wood makes it ideal for such work.

The wood needs no priming. The artist merely cleans it. Acrylics are preferred to oils because they are not absorbed as readily as other paints. Here, too, paint should be used sparingly so you do not lose the texture of the wood. You may sketch your design or picture with India ink and a quill pen or use a magic marker or any permanent, waterproof coloring pencils. Then, simply color in the design. Boards to be used for painting should be stored upright as they will warp if laid on the ground. If the wood is to be painted a solid color first to give it a canvas-like coat on which to compose, do it to both sides so that the piece of wood will dry evenly.

Collage on Wood

A natural combination is wood and paper, the marriage of the source and the product. Designs or full pictures may be torn or cut from any variety of glossy magazines on the market today. (When tearing a picture out to achieve a rough edge, hold the chosen piece in your hand, and tear the piece to be discarded down and away from you so as to leave the white edge on the discarded piece. Practice first on a scrap.) Paper may be glued to wood using any of the media suggested. When dry, your creation may be glazed with two or three coats of a matte or high gloss medium, whichever you prefer.

Pictures also may be transferred to light wood using a high gloss polymer medium, leaving only the ink behind. Apply a coat of the medium to the selected wood surface; allow it to dry. Apply a second coat to the wood and a coat to the face of the picture to be transferred. Mount the picture face down, making sure there is full contact by rolling the back with a pizza roller. Wet the back of the paper and allow it to dry until it is no longer cold to the touch. Then, apply water liberally to the back of the paper again, and, using your fingers, rub the paper off the wood. The ink is now permanently transferred to the wood.

Sculpture

Some found pieces may require only your recognition to become free-standing sculpture. Or you may mix several elements and add a base. To mount a wood sculpture on a wood base, drill or rout out a hole in the base to fit the contact point of the sculpture. Into it pour white glue and inset the sculpture. Set it aside to dry undisturbed for several days. Sculptures also may be attached to bases using dowel rods to give the illusion of suspension. Assembled pieces may represent figures, characters, dream images, nonsense, or humoresques. This art has a free form all its own.

Mobiles

The first recognized "mobile" was done by Alexander Calder in 1920. Since then, the form has become popular from amusements

"Sea Creatures" is a collection of found wood which suggests (from top to bottom) a dolphin, a ray (an actual shell), and a swimming turtle. The worm-eaten wood on the lower left has the look of coral and frayed rope suggests seaweed. (By the author.)

Polished driftwood floats in the breeze on a city porch.

for infants to a focus for daydreamers in office cubicles. To assemble a found-wood mobile you will need to collect an assortment of pieces of different shapes and approximately the same weight. Lay out the pieces in the way you would like them hung, planning their proximity so as to avoid confusion when they are in motion. Polish or paint each piece as you wish. Determine the balance point of the primary piece from which the others will hang by sticking a needle into various spots in the side of the wood until you find center. Using a tiny drill bit, bore holes through each piece at the point from which it is to be hung. Tie the

pieces together in a balanced design using fishing line. The mobile may be suspended from the ceiling inside or from a porch overhang outside. Table model mobiles may be made by using a large base with a raised arm from which smaller pieces may be suspended.

Wood Burning

The old scout art of wood burning, with an artist's eye and deft fingers, can turn plain wood into etchings fit for any viewing. The design may be drawn on the wood with India

Coconut "fur" and found wood suggests a bulky pelican. The metal loop at the bottom implies a fish hook. (By the author)

ink; then, using an inexpensive and easy-to-use wood burning pencil available at hobby and craft shops, burned into the wood itself. With pressure to the side of the pencil you can make broad strokes and with quick, light touches of the tip make fine etch marks to contrast. You may wish to work on scrap wood until you become adept.

Wood Artists and Their Work

"Woods of Wisconsin":   Dressed in a red plaid logging shirt and a camouflage-colored duck-billed hat, Wayne Konkle sat making clocks for art browsers at the Woodstock, Illinois, art fair in May, 1978. A shop teacher in southern Wisconsin during the school year and a summer house painter, Konkle uses his aerial bucket truck to get to the out-of-reach burls on apple, juniper, walnut, maple, willow, and other Wisconsin trees. He also entreats woodsfolk and neighbors to "spare that tree" so he may pursue his hobby of making clocks, bowls, and pen sets from the uniquely grained wood warts.

Burls are the best for providing the abstract grains seen in his delicate bowls and

on the faces of highly polished clocks. He also uses tree roots and the grain from the crotches of trees.

Following the removal of the burl and its bark, it takes Konkle about six to seven hours of work on a power lathe to make his paper-thin serving pieces. After sanding them smooth, he applies an FDA-approved epoxy sealant, making the bowls art to eat out of.

Touch of the Earth: Karilia and Tim Lipsker of Barrington, Illinois, are picking up the pieces. Those that look good to them they think will appeal to others as well, es-

"Wood of Wisconsin," the art of Wayne Konkle, looks more like fine grained stone than a polished burl.

Found forest wood forms the base for sprouting mushrooms, the art of Karilia and Tim Lipsker.

pecially after their tender touches. After selecting forest finds from Michigan, Wisconsin, Illinois, and other territories, the couple proceeds to clean, dry, and buff the gnarled woods.

"They are so pretty the way they are, we don't really need to touch them," Tim remarks.

Knots are knocked out and backed with mirrors, and crafted mushrooms appear as though they grew naturally among the waves and curves of the wood. Made of the roots of upturned or riverbed oaks, the prepared mushroom heads are mounted using flexible electrical wire which allows the Lipskers to bend and group the oak root mushrooms the way they grow on the forest floor.

"They're pretty; they're something we have made, and it's a good feeling when people like the pieces for what they are . . . natural."

That which is art to one and craft to another may have once been born of necessity by the originator. The following examples of "art" come from the everyday work-and-play lives of the Indians.

Bark Craft

Using the barks of the elm, hickory, pine, poplar, cottonwood, white cedar, spruce, hemlock, and, of course, the birch, the Indians made all kinds of things. You may follow suit by using the bark of blown down trees or those which have been knocked over at building sites. Strip the bark from the tree trunk using your knife and work it off straight on the grain with wedges so as not to break complete and workable pieces. To carry it back to camp or home, roll the bark *against* the grain if possible. If it resists and

Found forest wood forms the base for sprouting mushrooms, the art of Karilia and Tim Lipsker.

threatens to crack, roll it naturally. Back at your work area, roll it out flat on the ground and weight it with logs. If it is dry, pour hot water over it to make it flexible. Soak the bark in hot water, then scrape it to remove the rough outer bark, and scrub it to remove the resin. The tools you will likely need to make the following bark items are a sharp knife, scissors, an awl or another type of hole punch, and a darning needle.

Bark Book Cover: Using birch or elm, cut a piece of bark at least 1 inch (2.5cm) larger than the book you wish to cover. Cut a flap piece the same height as the book and 3 inches (7.5cm) wide. Score and punch holes ½ inch (12.7mm) apart and ½ inch in all around the cover. Punch corresponding holes on one length and both widths of the flap. Lace the flaps to the cover with pliant evergreen roots or inner bark fiber, and slip the book into its new cover.

Bark duck decoy

Bark Ducks: Originally decoys, bark ducks may be made easily by camp children. Trace a silhouette of any duck type—wood, pintail, or old squaw, for example—on a flattened piece of bark. Cut it out with scissors. Make a float of a sapling segment 3 inches (7.5cm) long and 2 inches (5cm) in diameter by slitting it with a knife or saw. Insert the bark duck forms and glue with waterproof glue. Now simply set them sailing.

Hatbands: To give your camp cap a woodsy look, take a strip of bark 2½ inches (6cm) wide and long enough to fit around your hat (with sufficient overlap). You may lace the ends together and finish the edges

Bark hat band

the same way as the book cover, or you may slit the band vertically near one end and whittle an arrow point on the other. Latch them together by inserting the arrow into the slit at the opposite end.

Whistle: Want to make your own call of the wild, or keep the kids in audio range? Here is a useful whistle suggested to serve the purposes. Take heavy paperlike birch bark and cut out a pattern like the one

Bark whistle for calling birds and kids

shown above. Score the middle and fold; then, score and bend the ends to form the whistle "lips." Blow, but do not be surprised if the only thing you catch with this whistle is a scolding from the birds.

Block Printing

Block printing was used by the Indians to decorate their clothes, identify their belongings, and beautify themselves. The Algonquin Indians whittled soft basswood (or the root of the jack-in-the-pulpit) into their own designs. Juices from berries or nuts were used as is or prepared as dyes by boiling them in water. A mullein leaf was used like a stamp pad to absorb the color, and the wood design was pressed into it to draw out the dye. Then the design was transferred to skin or any flat material with a distinctive marking.

Dyes: Various berries, fruits, roots, or whole plants provide a wide spectrum of natural colors which may be used for block printing:

Red—cherries, strawberries, raspberries,

sorrel, red oak, hemlock bark, bloodroot (straight)

Red-violet—dandelion roots

Red-purple—pokeweed

Rosy-tan—birch, willow bark, sassafras root

Salmon—cherry bark

Blue—blueberries

Violet—grapes

Green—plantain leaves and roots, nettle

Yellow—goldenrod flowers, osage orange roots and bark, St. John's wort

Yellow-orange—bloodroot (boiled)

Dark brown—walnut husks (boiled)

Black—walnut husks, sumac leaves

Jack-in-the-pulpit

To prepare, chop the plant or bark into fine pieces and soak it overnight. Simmer for one hour and strain the liquid through cheese cloth.

Cat Kewpies

Chippewa children had dolls to play with just as other children do. First they had to make them. Full-grown cattail rushes were

Kewpie Kutie

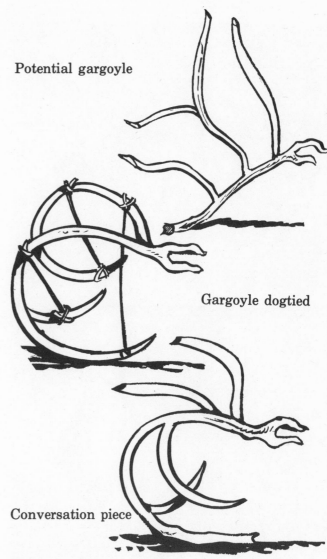

Potential gargoyle

Gargoyle dogtied

Conversation piece

cut, allowed to dry in the sun, and then momentarily soaked in water. A number of rushes then were taken and folded in half together and tied 1 inch (2.5cm) below the fold with a fiber cord. A shorter bunch of rushes were inserted for arms and a second fiber cord tied at the "waistline." The bottom tails were fanned out to form a skirt.

Papoose Pack for Dolls

Taking a young sapling with a long fork, lash the tines of the fork together in a hoop effect. The hoop is then crossed with additional numbers of sticks which are lashed to it. The doll, like a live papoose, is held on the frame with crisscrossed bark thongs and carried on the back with arm loops.

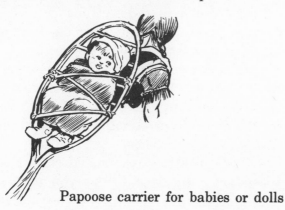

Papoose carrier for babies or dolls

Root Art

Freeform, abstract, three-dimensional root art is a simple way to make your own gargoyles! Simply take the fallen branch of a sapling—preferably one with many offshoots—and tie the shoots to one another in unusual combinations and bends. Submerge the bound branch in water for 24 hours; remove and let it sun dry. When the cords are cut, the branches will have taken on a new form. Hang it on a patio, set it on a coffee table as a conversation piece, or use it as a candle mount. You will never see another one like it.

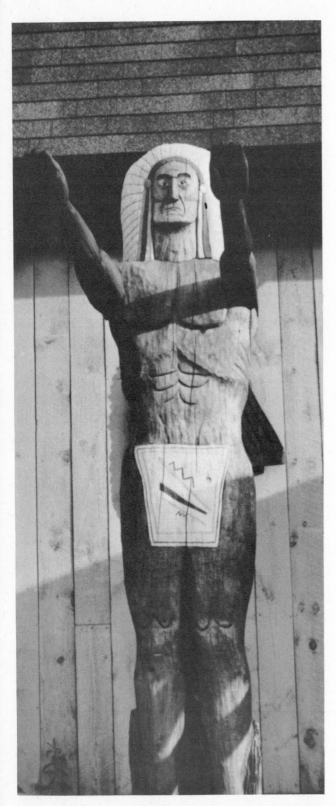

A great wooden Indian offers the blessing of the Great Spirit to passers-by.

Sketch Art

Burnt sticks are more than old firewood. They are a means to quick art and a good way to spend an outdoor afternoon. To prepare charcoal drawing sticks burn the ends of thin, close-grained hardwood twigs, about the size of pencils, in the campfire. Cover the fire with earth to squelch the flames. This lets the sticks heat through. Remove them and sharpen them on a piece of flat sandstone. You may draw on whatever is available, adding shadings with a dried mullein leaf and erasing your mistakes with a ball of fresh bread.

Painting also may be done using the natural dyes mentioned before. You may make a brush by chewing the end of a hickory twig to make the brush bristles. Comb the bristles to straighten them and trim across with your knife to make them even. You may hold your dyes in a clam shell and paint on bark or newspaper. Using the same dyes, you may even finger paint. Your nails make the sharp lines of detail and the tips of your fingers provide the soft, broad lines and shadings.

Totems

Totem poles were created by the Indians of the Northwest Coast—the Chilkat, Kwakietl, Salish, Nŏotka, Haida, and others. They depicted mythical creatures, deceased relatives, and animals, among other things. The softwoods—red cedar, spruce, soft pine, willow, cottonwood, basswood, aspen, white pine, hemlock, and tulip—form the bases of the totem art. Those logs which were green and contained the fewest knots were best.

The special tools needed to carve a large totem are a lumberman's crayon, a wood mallet, chisels ½, 1, and 1½ inches (12.7mm,

The Spirit moves David Tengren and the head of a horse tops a totem.

For five years, a New England man has been making up myths in 16-foot lengths. David Tengren of Norton, Massachusetts, is a totem builder. Using mallet, chisel, and gouge, he whacks and whittles the Northern White Pine poles of southern New England into snakes, beavers, eagles, turtles, and other animals. He also uses antique tools such as a draw knife, bark spud, adz, and broad ax to render totems out of trees.

"It's like cartooning," he says of his work, which started when he attended an art show. Like many other browsers at such fairs who say, "I could do that—and better," David did and does. He began by making up wood signs for friends and local businesses using a set of birthday-gift tools, and he soon graduated to cigar store Indians, life-size (and then some) Vikings, and, finally, full totems, which he admits are " the most fun."

Each pole takes him about 120 hours of work from the first design to the last lick of paint. Each animal or other figure is allotted a 3-foot (.9m) long cylinder. Working accord-

2.5 and 3.75cm) in diameter, a hand ax, and 1 to 1½ inch (2.5-3.75cm) gouges. Using the hew line and notch method described in Chapter 2, smooth one side of a fallen log (remove about ⅓ of the surface). De-bark the rest. On the prepared surface paint the main features of the design in a light color or draw them with charcoal and rough-cut the design with an ax. Details and finer features may be added with mallet and chisels. The totem may be painted with commercial paints in bright colors or dyed with vegetable or root dyes.

Miniature totems of 3, 5, and 10 inches (7.5, 12.5 and 25cm) are easily made of balsa or soft white pine using a pencil, a coping saw, and a sharp knife. The process consists of outlining figures from a side view and cutting out the details with a small saw or knife. The tiny totem design is then outlined in black and painted with water colors, oils, or acrylics.

David Tengren's totems and animal silhouettes are the atmospheric decor at Ann's Place, a lakeside restaurant in Norton, Massachusetts.

A farm family poses post perfect and stock still where David Tengren planted the grouping at Ann's Place, Norton, Massachusetts

ing to what the customer wants and what he envisions in a pole himself, Tengren sees a totem as a success if "what comes out pleases me and pleases the customer."

At 30, Tengren still has lots of totem time ahead of him to develop his art. And lots of quiet friends to keep him company.

Games

Hoop and Arrow Game: Make a hoop of a willow sapling bent into a circle (heating it with hot water to ease it into a bend, if necessary). Lash the overlapped ends and weave the inner space of the circle with thongs. Make an arrow out of a straight stick with an attached arrowhead or nail at one end and feathers or whittled wood wings at the other. The game is played by one player rolling the hoop while another one tries to knock it over with the arrow. The game advances one point at a time.

Hoop and arrow game

Indian Stick Game: Another simple game is played with two flat-sided sticks. One side is left blank and the other is painted or carved with drawings. The sticks are thrown into the air together and the player gains a point if both land with the pictures upward.

Stick 'n' ball game

Darts and Balls: Sharpen one end of a thin stick to a point and push it through a 3-inch (7.5cm) corn cob. You may attach feathers to the end opposite the point to acquire balance. To make a ball, cover a wad of grass or cotton with a thin piece of cloth. Stitch. The game is played by a circle of players. The ball is dropped into the center, and the dart is passed from one to the other. In turn, each player tries to stick the ball with the dart. The play advances one point at a time. (More complex rules and points may be developed by more competitive players.)

If art is in the eye of the beholder, look around. You may discover a lost form or create a new one. The forest holds many surprises.

Bibliography

Adney, Edwin Tappan, *Bark Canoes and Skin Boats of North America,* Howard I. Chappelle, 1964. Includes photos and construction drawings of watercraft of North American Indians; materials, tools, form, step-by-step pictures. Available through the Superintendent of Documents, U.S. Government Printing Office, Washington, D.C. 20402 ($6.75).

Angier, Bradford, *Skills for Taming the Wilds,* Stackpole Books, Harrisburg, PA, 1967.

Angier, Bradford, *Taming the Wilds,* Galahad Books, NY, 1967.

Angier, Bradford, *Wilderness Gear You Can Make Yourself,* Collier Books, NY, 1973.

Beard, D.C., *Shelters, Shacks, Shanties,* Charles Scribners' Sons, New York, 1914. This book is for real wilderness purists; it illustrates the construction of on-site objects from found materials using ax, crosscut saw, hammer, and rope. Design drawings included.

Bohm, Hansi, *Making Simple Constructions,* Watson-Guptill Publications, New York, 1972.

Brockman, C. Frank, *Trees of North America,* Golden Press, New York, 1968.

Burke, Edmund H., *Camping Handbook,* Arco Publishing Co., New York, 1955.

Canoe Poling, A.S. Barnes and Co., Inc., Cranbury, NJ.

Colby, C.B. and Angier, Bradford, *The Art and Science of Taking to the Woods,* Stackpole Books, 1970.

Elman, Robert, *Discover the Outdoors,* The Lion Press, Inc., NY, 1969.

Esslen, Rainer, *Back to Nature in Canoes,* Columbia Publishing Co., Inc., Frenchtown, NJ, 1976.

Explorers Ltd. Source Book, The, Harper & Row, 1977 (revised).

Fisher, Timothy, *Huts, Hovels and Houses,* Addison-Wesley Publishing Co., Reading, MA, 1977.

Graves, Richard, *Bushcraft: A Serious Guide to Survival and Camping,* Warner Books, 1978.

Henderson, Luis M., *Campers' Guide to Woodcraft and Outdoor Life,* Dover Publications, Inc., NY, 1972.

Jaeger, Ellsworth, *Nature Crafts,* Macmillan Co., NY, 1956.

Jaeger, Ellsworth, *Wildwood Wisdom,* Macmillan, NY, 1950.

Jensen, Charles L., *Lightweight Backpacking,* Bantam Books, NY, 1974.

Kephart, Horace, *Camping and Woodcraft,* Macmillan, NY, 1917.

Knobel, Bruno, *101 Camping-Out Ideas and Activities,* Wilshire Book Co., No. Hollywood, CA, 1961.

Laubin, Reginald and Gladys, *The Indian Tipi—Its History, Construction and Use,* Ballantine Books, Inc., NY, 1957. Plans for construction, set-up and furnishing of Sioux and other Indian housing.

McPhee, John, *The Survival of the Bark Canoe,* Farrar, Straus, Giroux, NY, 1975.

Mason, Bernard S., *Camping Crafts,* A.S. Barnes & Co., Cranbury, NJ, 1973.

Mason, Bernard S., *Woodcraft,* A.S. Barnes & Co., 1973.

Meilach, Dona A., *Box Art: Assemblage and Construction,* Crown Publishers, Inc., NY, 1975.

Norbeck, Oscar E., *Indian Crafts for Campers,* Association Press, NY, 1967.

Ormond, Clyde, *Complete Book of Outdoor Lore, Outdoor Life,* Harper & Row, NY, 1964.

Petrides, George A., *A Field Guide to Trees and Shrubs,* Houghton Mifflin Co., Boston, MA, 1958 (1972).

Rossman, Wm., *Builders of Birch Bark Canoes,* The Chicagoland Canoe Base, Inc., 4019 N. Narragansett Ave., Chicago, IL 60634. Methods of building bark canoes; Chippewa and voyageur design.

Riviere, Bill, *Backcountry Camping,* Doubleday & Co., Inc., Garden City, NY, 1971.

Riviere, Bill, *The Camper's Bible,* Doubleday & Co., Inc., Garden City, NY, 1961.

Schneider, Richard C. *Crafts of the North American Indians, A Craftsman's Manual,* Van Nostrand Reinhold Co., NY, 1972.

Sloane, Eric, *A Reverence for Wood,* Funk & Wagnalls, NY, 1965.

Sommer, Elyse and Mike, *Creating with Driftwood and Weathered Wood,* Crown Publishers, Inc., NY, 1974.

Taggart, Jean E., *Motorboat, Yacht or Canoe—You Name It,* The Scarecrow Press, Inc., Metuchen, NJ, 1974.

Weaver, Robert W., and Merrill, Anthony F., *Camping Can Be Fun,* Harper & Brothers, NY, 1948.

Wigginton, Eliot, ed., *The Foxfire Book,* Anchor Books, Garden City, NY, 1972.

Index